NETWORKING IN THE VIRTUAL AGE

CONNECTING WITH NO LIMITS

William M. Saleebey, Ph.D.

Book Design by HMDpublishing

Published by Insight Media

ISBN: 978-1-7360090-0-0 (Paperback)

ISBN : 978-1-7360090-1-7 (Ebook)

Table of Contents

Foreward 8

Remembrance 10

Dedication 11

Acknowledgments 12

Testimonials 14

Why I Wrote this Book 19

Participant-Observer: Nature of My Research 22

Section 1. INTRODUCTION

My Networking History: A Perspective 26

Things We Used to Do 32

Major Differences Between Virtual and In-Person
Networking 34

Section 2. ZOOM BASICS

Zoom is the Word: My Experiences with Virtual
Conferencing 42

Zoom Functionality and Essentials 44

Zoom Etiquette 48

Paying Attention During Meetings 50

Chat Awareness 52

What's Behind You? 53

Breakout Rooms 54

Zoom & Geography 56

Combatting Zoom Fatigue 57

Section 3. VIRTUAL NETWORKING

Making a Virtual Impact 60

Virtual Introductions (Elevator Speeches) 61

Virtual Troikas 63

Virtual Happy Hours...Make Them Happy 66

Leading Virtual Networking Meetings:
Requisite Skills 67

Challenges and Successes of Leading Zoom
Networking Meetings 69

Key Virtual Networking Tips 71

Section 4. PSYCHOLOGY

Psychological Concepts/Skills for Networking . . . 76

Circadian Rhythms: Time and Networking 78

Time and Networking 81

The Influence of Age and Stage 83

Versatility and Relationships 85

Humor - Ya gotta laugh 87

The Dangers of Stereotypes. 89

Self-Perception and the Perception of Others. . . . 91

Roles and Their Influence 93

Primacy and Recency: Serial Position Effect 96

Freeing and Binding Questions: Toward Better
Communication. 98

Report Talk and Rapport Talk 100

Self-Disclosure 102

Introversion and Extroversion. 103

Nexus Concept 105

Group Dynamics 106

Conformity: Impact on Group Behavior. 108

Networking Norms 110

Strengths Perspective: Application
to Networking 112

Section 5. NETWORKING BASICS

Wide/Deep Networking Revisited:
What Has Changed 116

Testimonials and the Role of Gratitude
in Networking 118

Get Involved. 120

If You Don't Schmooze, You Lose 121

Relationship Building in One-on-One Meetings . . 123

Section 6. CASE STUDIES

Case Study - Mike the Lawyer 128

Case Study - Zelda the Zoomer 130

Case Study - Bob the Group Leader 131

Case Study - Justin the Newbie 132

Case Study - Nancy the Hugger. 133

Case Study - Phil the Extrovert Techie 135

Section 7. KEY QUESTIONS

What's Your Goal?. 138

Do We Need to Meet in Person? 140

How Important is Convenience? 142

The Organization or the Person?. 143

How Important is that Call?. 145

What Channel Are You On?. 147

How Can We Use Different Channels
to Reconnect with Others? 149

Cliques...or Bonding?. 153

Section 8. SOCIAL MEDIA

Harnessing the Value of Social Media 156

LinkedIn Basics 161

How to Communicate on LinkedIn 170

Section 9. APPLICATIONS AND THE FUTURE

Virtual Meetings: Other Groups 186

Rotary Club 188

Book Club 189

Mah Jongg. 191

Virtual Networking Meetings: The Future. 192

Unique Time in History 195

Conclusion. 196

Also by William M. Saleebey 198

Biography 199

APPENDICES 201

Foreward

Dr. Bill Saleebey has done it again. In his latest treatise on networking, *Networking in the Virtual Age*, he has cleverly blended the newer Zoom Era with how it used to be — in-person meetings. In addition to covering all of the basics of building relationships via networking, he has laid out a roadmap for how to maximize your experience with Zoom.

Bill challenges us to rethink our prior ways of networking, yet remain true to ourselves. Sincerity and empathy capture the moment, and are the cornerstones of business contacts. He urges each of us to dig deep within oneself and find the real you. That is the person to present, whether in person or on Zoom. He encourages us to create new ways to be memorable and distinguish our services, so we are not lost in the Zoom clutter.

If you care and share, you will succeed in any environment. Your love/hate feelings about Zoom are shared by many. Dr. Bill shows us how to get past the fatigue and build lasting relationships. While no one knows the exact nature of future networking, this book is an important read to cope with the now and excel in the future.

Davis Blaine
Founder, Provisors
Founder, Legacy Forum
Chairman, Mentor Securities LLC

Remembrance

This book pays homage to the memories of the many victims of COVID-19 and their families and friends. The loss of their lives is tragic. However, we can take some solace in knowing that despite the devastation, our resulting physical distancing has demonstrated that we as social beings are determined to connect with others even when we can't meet in person.

Dedication

I would like to dedicate this book to my late cousin Dennis Saleebey, aka Beez, who was a huge inspiration to me throughout my life. Dennis was an originator of the Strengths Perspective, a seminal movement in the field of social welfare. He dedicated his career to developing the wise principle that we need to look at people's strengths to find a route to their success.

Dennis was brilliant, funny and kind. He always encouraged me and was an outstanding role model. He continues to be the most famous Saleebey and leads the Google search for our unusual last name. Thanks Beez for leading the way. Your guidance and friendship have had a monumental influence on my life and career.

Acknowledgments

Writing a book is a truly collaborative effort. I couldn't have and didn't do it alone. Many people were part of the process and deserve special acknowledgment.

First and foremost, my son Billy Samoa Saleebey was with me every step of the way. He provided much needed feedback, contributed mightily to the section on social media and LinkedIn, and did most of the work on publication and promotion of the book. He was my right-hand person, and I couldn't have done this without him. He also co-wrote the section on LinkedIn.

Leah Malecha, Membership Coordinator of Bruin Professionals and copy editor of the book, contributed many ideas and was instrumental in the publication and promotion of the book.

The following people read early drafts of the book and made valuable contributions. They include Eddie Neiman, Ken Chong, Keith Gregory, Marc Swan, Regina Lark, Matt Crisafulli, Rod Ponce, Nancy Davis, Bob Green, and David MacGillivray.

Interviews were integral to the content of the book. Networking group management who shared critical information about their organizations' response to the pandemic include Matt Toledo (Provisors), Ken Chong (Bruin Professionals), Forrest Blake (Highrise Networks), Justin Blaine (Athletes Touch), Eric Shaw (All Cities Resource Group), Travis Sims (Accelerated Global Connections), Ivan Misner (BNI), Jeri and Brian Hemsworth (Echelon), Jeff Krumholz (The Exchange), Joe Chatham (USA 500 Clubs) and Dotty Kaminsky (Provisors). They all contributed their ideas and insights willingly and openly.

A special thanks to Jay Abbasi for his contributions and co-writing the LinkedIn section.

Group Leaders who shared insights were Ivy Rappaport, John Celic, and Robbie Klein.

Other interviewees who shared insights were Nancy Davis, Justin Silverman, Philip Pfeifer, and Matt Soroky.

My partner Judy Moore was extremely supportive of the process and contributed her opinions and experiences with Zoom.

Testimonials

If you read any of Dr. Bill Saleebey's books and follow his suggestions on networking and building relationships, you will get more business, build stronger relationships and have fun doing it. His advice is simple, straightforward and practical. His latest book, *Networking in the Virtual Age* will either make you laugh at how people show up to virtual meetings or make you pause and think about how you have appeared on screen.

Kenneth M. Chong

President, Bruin Professionals

Dr. Bill is the guru of networking. This is his third book on networking, and it couldn't come at a better time when we are trying to adapt to a new model of business networking during this COVID-19 pandemic. He gives us very insightful suggestions from lighting, to facial expressions, and everything in between in order to optimize one's own virtual presence.

Nancy Davis

President, Davis Insurance Agency

Timeliness can be the key to creating meaningful change. Early on, Dr. Bill Saleebey identified the virtual networking need in this time of significantly impacted social contact. He has developed an action plan to keep our connection presses running. It starts with this how-to book on navigating Zoom in your networking life along with updated skills and strategies for enhancing communication in a virtual world. As Dr. Bill says, "Instead of lamenting the changes, take an honest look at the positive aspects of virtual networking." The future is now and we need to be ready and able to move with it.

Marc Swan

Vocational Counselor, Freelance Writer/Poet

Dr. Bill, whose expertise in the field of networking and psychology is critically acclaimed, has hit it out of the park again! His new book is perfect for the times. Whether you are an experienced networker or a novice, there is plenty of information, practical tips, and guiding cues throughout the book that can be learned and refined.

As a residential mortgage broker, networking is key to my business. I enjoyed this read, learned some critical things about virtual networking and felt energized about maintaining and strengthening my own networking skills. This is a timely book, especially in the era of COVID-19.

Eddie Neiman

Castle Funding Corp.

Dr. Saleebey's latest book has been a lifeline for me in my consulting business. He's a brilliant writer and addresses head-on the current need to understand how best to connect virtually. His case studies are particularly helpful. This is a must-read for anyone wanting to improve on 21st century communication skills.

Joan Lounsbery

Joan Lounsbery Management Services

Networking in the Virtual Age by Dr. Bill Saleebey is an essential read for anyone networking in the "post-COVID" era. It highlights the challenges and limitations of meeting virtually, rather than in-person, and presents a clear philosophy for gaining traction in this fluid environment.

The book identifies the basics of effective networking in a traditional sense and explains how they translate to the present day world of virtual meetings. Case studies are used to demonstrate how the goals of either "wide" or "deep" networking can be achieved in different situations. Best practices in the use of social media, and most particularly LinkedIn, are discussed in remarkable detail, enabling the reader to make the best possible choices in virtual and in-person arenas alike.

No one can predict exactly how networking will evolve after COVID restrictions are lifted, but as Dr. Bill explains, we are likely to be faced with some aspects of virtual networking for a long time. Anyone serious about referrals will need to adapt to this new reality. Dr. Bill's book provides the insight for anyone to flourish in this environment.

Bob Green

Vice President of Membership, Bruin Professionals

I consider myself a professional networker and I feel like a know-it-all, smarty pants when it comes to the subject. But it wasn't until I read Dr. Bill Saleebey's *Networking in the Virtual Age* that I realized that yes, digital networking in the age of the Zoom room, is an art unto itself. Here's what I appreciated about this useful volume. First, the book presents useful tools for all types of virtual networking, from social media to Zoom meetings. Secondly, *Networking in the Virtual Age* provides real time glimpse into networkers' response of COVID-19 social distancing, and useful advice on Zoom functionality and etiquette. Finally, Dr. Saleebey provides a clear comparison of virtual and in-person networking, which helps the reader make a quick shift from one modality to the other with ease. It's a great book, easy to read, and recommended to anyone who understands the importance of developing the skills to make great connections with potential clients, mentors, and friends.

Regina F. Lark, Ph.D.

CEO, A Clear Path

This is an extremely timely book that clearly details how to network successfully in this period of virtual everything. Bill Saleebey takes us on a brief tour of his own networking history to illustrate that it takes hit and misses to develop a sound networking approach.

His coverage of Zoom and how virtual networking is an art is well developed. The section on "psychology" is critical to how we perceive ourselves and how others perceive us. And, most importantly, he gives us a blueprint on how we can control our own narrative and therefore control how we are perceived.

The case studies were quite illuminating and his discussions on various social media, in particular, LinkedIn was excellent.

This is a book that covers all the bases of networking in this virtual age and should be a "must read" for anyone trying to navigate a networking presence.

George Poulakos

Managing Partner, Tribeca Communications

This book is clear, concise, and included all the important stuff (no fluff). It was a short read, and was enjoyable the entire time. I particularly liked reading more about the author's networking history at the beginning and I also enjoyed the case studies of professionals at the end of the book.

The content is extremely timely, and the nuances about Zoom meetings are so relevant. It was a pleasure reading this networking masterpiece!

Rod Ponce

President Elect, Bruin Professionals

Why I Wrote this Book

I am a member of two networking groups, Provisors and Bruin Professionals. In addition, I have been a member of others and spoken to many groups about the networking process and networking skills.

I have written two previous books on networking, *Connecting: Beyond the Name Tag* (2009) and *Connecting: Key Networking Tips for Business and Life* (2016). Both of my previous networking books, and my prior networking presentations, were written when the norm for most people was in-person networking. Zoom existed, but the vast majority of people didn't use the platform for any personal or business use.

This book is different. It was inspired by the dramatic and life-changing COVID-19 pandemic, which propelled into Los Angeles in March of 2020 and shut down in-person meetings. Networking groups I was involved in quickly pivoted and started offering Zoom meetings as the norm.

Here is what happened. On Friday, March 13, 2020, Governor Gavin Newsom issued a "shelter in place" order for the state of California. It happened suddenly, and no one had any idea, or was thinking, "What about our networking groups?" We learned shortly thereafter that we would be using Zoom to hold virtual meetings. My networking groups hastily trained Group Leaders and members on how to utilize Zoom, and the whole landscape changed at that point. We needed to pivot, and pivot we did.

Few people had been previously trained on how to run or attend a Zoom networking meeting. It was new to almost everyone. As in most sudden changes, some people adapted more quickly than others.

There was much more guesting at groups outside of people's geographic area. People purchased cameras for computers that didn't have them, stacked books under their computer to get the camera eye level, and cleaned up their backgrounds so they looked more professional. They learned basic Zoom functionality and protocol, and adjusted to virtual networking meetings.

Attendance proliferated and geography ceased to be a barrier to attending meetings. A leader of a Bruin Professionals group asked me to speak at his meeting. I agreed to do so, and decided that my upcoming presentation needed to address our current situation, not the way things were. I developed an entirely new presentation with visuals, and delivered it for the first time on July 2. It went well. People were definitely interested in this very relevant topic.

I got sick in mid-July and decided to get a COVID-19 test. I had serious thoughts about my mortality as the number of fatalities continued to rise, and considered writing a book about what was happening around me. (By the way, I tested negative for COVID-19.)

A day later, after genuine reflection, I decided to write another book that addressed networking during and possibly after the pandemic, and the social distancing that it requires. This book is time-sensitive, and was written in mid-August 2020 about things as we have been experiencing them, and the real time changes that the various networking groups and chapters are making to adapt to the pandemic.

In general, it is important for a book to stand the test of time. I am fully aware that things won't be the way they are now, and I make no apology for that. I know that things will be different and do not claim to accurately predict the future.

I am a seasoned networker, steeped in Psychology, who also leads networking groups and has an influence in the future of them. This especially applies to Bruin Professionals, where I have been on the Board of Directors for over 14 years. Thus, I have various roles that make me uniquely qualified to write about this topic.

My goal in this book, as in all of my books, is to say things as I see them, and try to assist others as much as possible in navigating this unique time by providing useful tips and skills that are immediately applicable.

Participant-Observer: Nature of My Research

This book is based primarily on my observations and interviews with a wide variety of networkers and networking groups. Being a participant-observer is engaging in legitimate research. In participant-observation, researchers become active participants in the situation they are studying.

As I participated, observed and discussed the pivot and transition from in-person to virtual meetings, I realized that what we were experiencing was new and unprecedented. No one really knew where everything was going to go.

As a participant, I had mixed feelings about Zoom vs. in-person meetings. I really like people, and am not averse to a firm handshake, fist bump, or hug. But that choice was gone for the time being, and I knew I had to adapt.

I learned how high to place the computer, how to get proper lighting, and how to quickly find the mute button.

I was mastering the medium, and not really missing or longing for the food-filled conference rooms of recent February.

I was pleased to not be sitting in traffic and standing in lines at Security. I could wake up later. I was in no hurry to return to the way things were, and enjoyed the gift of more time.

As an observer, I noticed that people were attending meetings in "locations" that they hadn't before. Some seemed quite comfortable with the new channel, others not so much. I also observed the homes of people and learned a few interesting things about them, like how much a particular cat might dominate their lives, or that having a house full of hyper kids was no picnic.

To do participant-observation properly, it is vital to remain objective and to acknowledge your role in the process. It could be as a group member, a group leader, a guest at a group, or a leader of a networking organization.

INTRODUCTION

My Networking History: A Perspective

My formal history in business networking began in about 1985. I was working as a salesman for a moving company, and my sales manager told me that I needed to network to generate business. I asked, "What is that exactly?" He really didn't know networking as it is today and told me I needed to meet other vendors in businesses related to moving, such as real estate brokers, furniture dealers and architects, and exchange leads with them. Thus it began, without a huge amount of success. One of the people I met around that time was a commercial real estate broker named Forrest Blake. Commercial brokers did the leases of companies who were moving, and were a great potential referral source for me.

My lead exchange (it really wasn't much more than that) continued with moderate success for a few years. Around 1995, I got a call from Forrest asking to meet for coffee to chat about an idea he had for me. We met, and he told me about a networking group called All Cities that had a significant number of professionals who would meet monthly. I checked it out and decided to join. It should be noted that neither All Cities nor any of the other networking groups I subsequently joined had any other movers in them. Therefore, as long as people knew what I did, liked, and trusted me, I would get referrals.

I did indeed get a substantial number of referrals, and I was on my way. I was raw, unseasoned, and still knew very little about the networking process. I vowed to learn, and learn I did, meeting some great people along the way: lawyers of all types, accountants, bankers, financial advisors, and many other types of professionals. I was having fun and getting business!

In 2002, one of the members of All Cities, Randy Shein-bein, who knew I was a UCLA alum, approached me after a meeting and told me about a group he and a couple of other alums were forming called Bruin Professionals. UCLA alums had looked across town and realized the USC alums seemed to do a better job of networking and referring business to fellow Trojans than we Bruins did. I told Randy I was all in and went to the very first meeting of Bruin Professionals in 2002. Over time, I lost interest in All Cities, and preferred the environment and people in Bruin Professionals.

There was another large networking group which then went by the name of Professionals Network Group or PNG. It was well established and had a similar member-ship base as All Cities. I tried to join. Initially I was reject-ed. The reason given at the time was that I was a "ven-dor" and not a "trusted advisor" the group was seeking. I was distraught, and shared my disappointment with a couple of members. They knew me, my character, and my background, and that I was more than merely a ven-dor. One of them, Barry Kurtz, lobbied for me, and I got a second chance to join the Sherman Oaks chapter. The leader of Sherman Oaks, Robbie Klein, met me, liked me, and invited me to join his chapter, which I did in 2005. His comment was "It's not the profession that matters, it is the PERSON."

A few years later, after learning a lot about the networking process as a participant-observer, I decided to write a book about networking. As I was writing the book, I went to a Provisors meeting and was placed into a troika with the Managing Director of Provisors, Gordon Gregory. The third person was not able to attend, so I had a one-on-one with Gordon. What better time to broach the topic of my book with Gordon! He was very receptive to the idea. He encouraged me, providing the names of about a dozen Provisors members who he recommended that I talk to about my book. He indicated that they could provide additional insight into the process and Provisors. I was very thankful and interviewed each one of the people he recommended to me. Because of Gordon's exalted position in the organization, they were all quite responsive.

That was very helpful, and my book, *Connecting: Beyond the Name Tag,* was published in 2009. My involvement with both Provisors and Bruin Professionals increased, and over time, I became a Group Leader, Vice President of Chapter Development, and eventually the President of Bruin Professionals. In 2010, I was asked to lead a Provisors group in Downtown Los Angeles. I was becoming an expert in networking. This was a totally unplanned and unexpected occurrence, and nothing I had been officially educated or trained to do. I learned from experience.

Ideas about the networking process kept manifesting, and I decided to write a second book, *Connecting: Key Networking Tips for Business and Life*, in 2015. It was published in 2016.

When the pandemic began to peak in March, I had no idea it would lead to my third book on networking and my fifth book overall.

It should be noted that the type of networking that has informed my views on the topic involve monthly networking meetings (usually in conference rooms until COVID-19). The meetings are followed up by troikas, which are smaller groups that meet at a different time to get to know each other better. Bruin Professionals refers to them as Minis, but the concept is the same. If your networking group has a different format, most principles in this book will still apply.

The field of business networking is undergoing a sea change.

This new way of networking began of necessity, with no real road map or time frame about how long it was going to last. Zoom was the technology of choice, initiated by Provisors. The management of Provisors was kind and generous enough to share their methods with Bruin Professionals. Both groups had many people "attending" meetings in geographic areas that they wouldn't have gone in the past.

Initially there was a vast learning curve, and people were forced to learn the technology. It was a novelty, and people were adjusting. Group Leaders were figuring out how to run a virtual meeting. Many things were different, and people were discovering the importance of having a camera on their computer, adequate lighting, and a professional background. The pandemic raged throughout the country and world, and America's political leadership was slow to respond.

George Floyd's murder and the renewed focus on the Black Lives Matter movement was part of a very chaotic and sad period. In the midst of stay-at-home orders, social distancing and mask requirements, we became consumed with racial justice, the dismantling of Confederate monuments and flags, and the rising divide of political opponents.

We are clearly living in unique times. We have a deadly global pandemic, and louder than ever, calls for racial justice. I choose to focus on business networking because that is what I know, what I do, and has peaked my interest for over thirty-five years. Currently, as of mid-August, 2020, there are no in-person networking meetings. People in networking groups, while perhaps not preferring virtual networking, seem to be embracing and learning the new way to connect with others. There is no clear end in sight. As long as social distancing is being at least nominally enforced, there won't be the types of meetings that we attended as recently as February.

Networking group management is (or should be) considering how they will operate going forward. I am keenly interested in how and where our future meetings will be held.

I come at this from a few perspectives, and I want to make those clear from the outset. I started (with others) many of the current chapters of Bruin Professionals, so I know some things about running an organization. As a Group Leader, I am quite interested in what running a group will be like going forward. I am also a member of both Bruin Professionals and Provisors, and live in Ventura, which is a considerable physical distance from the groups I lead and attend. I am currently considering my desire to return to in-person meetings. I don't love driving, sitting in traffic or waiting in Security lines (who does?). I truly hope that both groups, Provisors and Bruin Professionals, thrive in the future, but I'm not certain how much in-person meetings are essential to that survival.

In fact, virtual meetings seem to have a better chance of survival, given the possibility of future pandemics.

I have significant training and experience in Psychology and hold a doctorate in Educational Psychology/ Counseling. In that light, I have been fascinated how "real" virtual meetings are. I truly feel like I have been in touch with the people in the various meetings that I have attended over the past several months, although I have not actually physically touched any of them. It seems like the real thing, so why do we need to meet in person? That question and potential answers are a central focus of this book.

Things We Used to Do

Prior to the COVID-19 pandemic, there were many things that we did related to attending in-person networking meetings.

For now, we are not doing them.

Physical Contact		
Shaking Hands	Hugging	Touching Others
Face-to-Face Communication		
Eating with Others	Drinking with Others	Smelling Others (good and bad smells)
Mingling	Telling Stories and Jokes	Having "side" Conversations
Logistics		
Getting up Early	Driving in Traffic	Riding Uber or Lyft
Taking Metro	Parking	Using Valet Parking
Going Through Security	Walking to, from, before and after Meetings	Checking In and Leaving Business Cards
Wearing a Name Tag	Sitting in a Crowded Room	Deciding Where to Eat
Splitting the Bill		Getting Hard Copy Troika/Mini Sheets

Many of them are not necessarily things we like doing, and can give pause if we have a choice of attending an in-person meeting when we are able to do so again, or attending the meeting virtually.

Major Differences Between Virtual and In-Person Networking

———

Until March of 2020, the main networking I had done, and I had done plenty, was face-to-face, in-person networking. I had only used Zoom a handful of times. Suddenly both of my networking groups were adopting a temporary virtual type of networking meeting via Zoom. Few members of either group considered this to be a permanent situation. Over six months later, there is no end in sight to the COVID-19 pandemic. Social distancing and mask wearing have become mandated and a way of life, at least in California.

Here are the major differences of in-person and virtual networking that I've observed:

In-person Networking	Virtual Networking
Transportation	
• Attendees would drive or take Uber/Lyft or public transportation to meetings, often in the early morning. • There was the possibility of carpool or train conversations that could really build great personal relationships. I used to really enjoy taking the Metro to our downtown meeting and chatting and joking with my friend Eddie along the way.	• Attendees wake up, brush their teeth, comb their hair, turn their computer on, and join the meeting. • There is no more community being built on the way to the meeting, since no transportation is required.
Attire	
• Attire and hygiene were important, especially in certain regions. • Attendees wore business attire, and tried to present themselves in the best light possible. • You could see how people dressed, styled their hair, what kinds of shoes and socks they wore, and whether they were short or tall.	• Only a nice shirt and hair semi-done are needed to look presentable on Zoom. • Everyone is the same height and weight on Zoom. I know a 7' tall financial advisor and a 5' tall real estate broker, and they are the same height on Zoom.

In-person Networking	Virtual Networking
Body Language	
• Body language is essential and a key communication tool for attendees.	• You don't get to see people move and express themselves with full bodily posture and motion.
Meeting Environment	
• There is more potential for things like brainstorming, problem solving, and sharing of ideas. • In a conference room, you can scan the room and different seats to see all of the attendees.	• Everyone is muted, so there is less dialogue. Attendees have a front row seat on Zoom; you don't have any control about who you are placed next to, over or under. • Synergy, when combined efforts and teamwork take place, is more difficult to achieve.

In-person Networking	Virtual Networking
Pre-meeting and Post-meeting Chitchat	
• People would greet each other, shake hands, possibly hug those with whom they were closer, and casually chat before the meeting. • Similarly, there was more chatting after the meeting as troikas were being scheduled.	• There is less pre-meeting or post-meeting chitchat. • Side conversations are lacking greatly. • There are no "parking lot conversations" that were so much a part of meeting in person.
Membership	
• Meeting in person is especially important to new or younger members. It is more difficult to build new relationships with people who you haven't met face-to-face.	• I have noticed that veteran members are more comfortable with the virtual format largely because they already know others and have established relationships with them.

Picture if you will...Four attractive people of various ages and genders, dressed up, hair styled, shoes shined, ties knotted, name tag in its proper place on the right side, walking to a networking meeting in Downtown Los Angeles. They are really looking forward to the hot coffee, sumptuous spread of food and camaraderie. They check in at Security together, and ride up in a crowded elevator to the 31st floor. It is February 26, 2020, at 7:25 a.m. That is an example of what networking groups looked like then.

Enter March 2020...

The various networking groups and chapters began holding Zoom meetings. Members could hit a link from their home office and join the meeting. People would only see their upper half.

As of mid-August 2020, the virus is still on the rise. The scientists concur that we are still in the first wave of the pandemic. Therefore, we really don't know if and when we will return to the way things were. Some people are unlikely to want to return to in-person meetings, especially if they can continue to attend them virtually. Some professional firms that host the meetings are currently considering a possible timetable for returning to hosting meetings. There are potential legal issues about assembling large groups without any social distancing, or serving food and drinks in an hygienic and safe manner.

There has been talk of having "hybrid" meetings, where the host allows a smaller number to attend in person, with the remainder attending virtually. How would this work? Group leaders would have to conduct meetings that included both live and virtual attendees. There seem to be more disadvantages to a hybrid format than upsides. The topic of hybrid meetings will be addressed in more detail elsewhere in the book. Another option for the future is to have groups alternate in-person and virtual meetings from month to month. This is a less than ideal option because it would likely lead to spotty attendance.

Because the future is so uncertain, it is more important than ever to be flexible and have an open mind. Those who are willing to accept new "normals" will be better able to adapt to whatever the future holds for us. Don't focus on how great things were in the past. Rather, look at the advantages of the current situation. Instead of

lamenting the changes, take an honest look at the positive aspects of virtual networking.

SECTION 2 -
ZOOM BASICS

Zoom is the Word: My Experiences with Virtual Conferencing

W hen I first heard about Zoom, I immediately thought of the nickname my nephews and nieces call me, Uncle Zoom Zoom. I got that moniker when my oldest nephew, Scot, called me that when he was learning to talk because I then was 20 years old, owned an MG sports car, and would zoom from place to place.

In mid-March 2020, I was informed that due to the spreading coronavirus (now known as COVID-19), we would temporarily be having our meetings via Zoom. Not being a techie, I became a bit concerned about getting a camera for my computer and downloading the Zoom app. I realized that my computer had a camera, and downloading was easy. That's all I knew at the time, and I had no idea whatsoever the longevity of this stay-at-home order or the impact it would have on networking groups specifically, and business in general.

It was a new experience for me. I had used FaceTime many times, which was very easy to use. I had used Skype a number of times, but never really liked it much. It was clunky, unreliable and had spotty sound quality.

On Wednesday, March 25, ready or not, I led a Zoom networking meeting prior to attending one. It was baptism by fire to be sure. But I jumped in with both feet.

Almost six months later, I am a veteran of Zoom calls, using the platform for networking, work, and occasions with family and friends. You name it, I have done many of them.

Surprisingly, it doesn't seem like it has been six months since I have seen some of the people in the flesh who are regulars on the Zoom calls. It's not the same as meeting in person, but there is a definite air of reality to it. Whether it is the clarity of the images, the fact that I already knew many of the people on the calls, or something else, it seems like "the real thing".

Actually, it is the real thing, just a different kind of connection. Their "name tag" is under their image on the screen. But their image is all there, their voice is how you remember it, and for now, this is all we have.

Currently, Zoom is still a novelty to many people. They might deem it temporary, not take it seriously, and long hopefully for the quick return of face-to-face meetings. However, if you are in business and plan to be working for awhile, it behooves you to become as proficient as possible in navigating Zoom.

Zoom Functionality and Essentials

———

This section focuses on your presence on Zoom and the basic functionality of Zoom technology that will allow the reader to join a virtual meeting with full confidence.

The Physical Space Around You

Adjust the height of the camera so that you are centered on the screen. You can do this by either raising the height of your computer or your chair. You can also adjust the computer monitor so that you are centered. The camera should directly face you, not look up or down at you.

You must be well lit! The simplest way is to have ample light coming at you, either by sitting by a window or shining lights toward you. Natural light is ideal, but real lights should be used if you don't have enough natural light. In dim light, you might look like you are in the Witness Protection Program, which is not a flattering appearance. Don't be overexposed with too much light. Get feedback from others about your appearance and fine tune as needed.

Your background is also very important. You have many choices for both real or virtual backgrounds. If you are using a real background, it should be uncluttered and represent who you are. It doesn't have to be your company name or logo, but that is an option. Virtual backgrounds offer many options, whether that is a makeshift office space or vacation spot you can explain in an icebreaker activity. You should carefully consider how each one might be perceived by others.

The way you present yourself is much more transparent on Zoom than in-person meetings. Your attire, hairstyle, and facial expressions should put you in the best light. If you don't want to keep staring at yourself, you can eliminate your self-view and hide yourself.

Zoom Functions

First of all, make sure that you have a strong internet connection. Without that, you won't be able to properly function on Zoom.

Secondly, check your name and edit if needed so that it properly represents YOU, not your email, your wife, or some other person who uses your computer. It is also useful to put your company name, title, or industry next to your name so people know what you do.

It's critical to understand and use the muting function. If you are in a meeting where all participants are muted, be prepared to unmute yourself when you are about to speak by having your cursor near the mute button. I recommend that you mute yourself when you are not speaking or don't want to be heard in order to avoid any unwanted sounds coming from you. You can use the space bar as a shortcut to unmute yourself for a short period of time.

The Chat function allows you to have conversations during the meeting, either with an individual or the group. Don't overuse this function! Be careful if you are directing your chat to an individual that you aren't chatting to the entire group. Chat can also be saved. This feature is especially useful for group leaders who aren't able to check Chat during the meeting, but want to be sure they are aware of what was said.

Turning off the Video function is useful when you don't want to be seen for a variety of reasons. You should use it if you are leaving your computer for any reason, rather than leaving the visual of your space without you. Having your name come on when you turn off your Video is okay, but a picture of you is better. You can even have fun with this and put up an older picture of you or some other variation.

Another area of current debate is whether or not to turn your Video off when there is a speaker or when you need to do something else during a meeting. One position is not to stop your Video except when you must leave the room. Another is that it is acceptable to stop your Video, especially in a large group or while a speaker is presenting.

As you are becoming more proficient and savvy with virtual networking, remember that you are on camera and others might be assessing your demeanor. Be aware of your facial expressions, and smile often. Gesture and express yourself with some level of animation when appropriate.

Remember that everything is amplified on Zoom. You are constantly on camera and should be conscious of that. Be aware that you are expressing your *brand* in everything you say and do. Be self-aware without becoming overly self-conscious.

Reactions allow you to show your appreciation, agreement, support and indicate that you are engaged in the meeting. Use as a positive response, but don't overuse.

Full Screen ("Brady Bunch") or Speaker View offer the option of being aware of the entire group or focusing on the speaker.

Breakout Rooms are a very useful option provided by Zoom technology. They are controlled by the host. Another section of the book will further discuss Breakout Rooms.

Another helpful feature of Zoom is the ability to take quick polls of the audience in terms of their opinions, experiences and other measurable dimensions. The polls are simple and efficient, and the results are available quickly.

Zoom Etiquette

The proper etiquette for Zoom is emerging as I write this book, and like any opinions on manners, people have widely varying points of view. In my six month stint as a Zoomer (in addition to being a Boomer), I have noticed several striking themes.

First of all, when Zoom networking meetings first started, they were a novelty. So people sometimes acted silly and proudly showed their pajamas, beards and unruly hair. Then gradually most people realized that they were in a business meeting, even though it was in their kitchen, with three bored kids and a spouse who wanted to use the computer.

When I gave my first Virtual Networking Zoom presentation, I was stunned to see that one of the attendees called from his bed, and seemed to think that there was nothing inappropriate or unusual about his location. If he reads this book, he will realize the error of his ways and that his behavior is in the "Don't do this" category.

Here is a list of Do's and Don'ts to guide your Zoom experience:

Do's	Don'ts
Do use basic manners and be aware that a Zoom meeting is a business meeting.	Don't eat or drink on camera.
Do use body language to convey encouragement and support, such as head nodding, smiling, or arm gestures.	Don't yawn, fidget unduly or do anything that communicates boredom, negativity or disgust.
Do dress appropriately; attire should be professional.	Don't show up in your pajamas.
Do be patient and wait your turn to speak, unmuting quickly and muting promptly when you are finished speaking.	Don't speak out of turn or at length unless indicated by the Zoom monitor or Group Leader.
Do keep your primary focus on the meeting and text minimally and only as necessary.	Don't multi-task in sight of the camera. If you must do something else during the meeting, do so off-camera and discreetly.
Do use the Chat function only as needed.	Don't use the Chat as a side show or assume everyone is looking at it or cares about your comings and goings.
Do be polite to others.	Don't say any comments that are racist, sexist or demeaning to others in any way.
Do turn off your Video if you leave your computer for any reason.	Don't leave your Video on when you are away from your computer.

Etiquette is important in this virtual environment, and attendees should be aware of this and follow rules accordingly.

Paying Attention During Meetings

W hen I attended and led networking meetings prior to the pandemic, I paid attention and expected attendees to do the same. There was no chatting, reacting, virtual clapping or other blatant form of multi-tasking. Zoom seems to encourage a certain amount of multi-tasking.

Some chatting and responding to chatting is expected as part of the norms of acceptable behavior during virtual meetings. However, I find it can be distracting and sometimes downright rude.

Etiquette norms are still being established as so many people are now conducting their meetings virtually. Attention to the main meeting should be encouraged, and attendees should be made aware of the inherent problems with excessive chatting and other forms of multi-tasking.

Though in-person meetings were not perfect in terms of maintaining the focus and attention of attendees, there was generally better focus. People were able to establish eye contact with others, and the group leader could command more attention in a uniform manner than is usual via Zoom.

Chat Awareness

―――

Be careful when you use the Chat function on Zoom.

Make 100% sure that when you intend on chatting privately, you aren't chatting to Everyone.

For example, when you want to say, "Big Head is being a jerk again" to your buddy, be sure it just goes to your friend and not to Everyone, where "Big Head" would see it.

Making those kinds of comments are not only rude, but also risky.

If in doubt, don't say it.

What's Behind You?

O ne of the main advantages of virtual networking is that it gives others the opportunity to observe your office or home office and see the trappings of your personal space. This provides others with additional insight into you, the way you live and work, and the things that are important to you personally.

For this reason, your background is VERY important, and you can actually place things there that you want others to see and comment on. You should be intentional and strategic in assembling your background.

It is useful to place objects there that you might want to talk about to give others a better idea of who you are and what you do in your spare time.

Your background is critical in branding yourself. Ask for feedback about your background from others, and change it periodically to keep it fresh and interesting. For example, you can place a book or picture in a prominent place that represents something about you. You can also get ideas from others who have striking backgrounds.

Breakout Rooms

Breakout rooms are a very valuable and integral aspect of Zoom technology.

They actually provide a cleaner and easier way to break people up into groups than in-person meetings, primarily due to a sense of privacy and lack of noise interference.

In order to maximize the effectiveness of breakout rooms, it is important to quickly select a facilitator for the group discussion. This will allow everyone to participate and keep on topic. Someone can volunteer, or you can simply select the person whose first name begins with a letter that comes first in the alphabet.

If your group is going to report their results to the large group, you should select a scribe who will take notes, summarize the opinions of the group, and report the major points made in the breakout room to the main group.

Be a good listener, be patient, and wait for your turn to speak. In addition to attentively listening, contribute to the discussion. Stay on point and build on what others say.

The value of breakout rooms can be affected by the size of the group, the complexity of the topic, and the amount of time allotted. From a psychological perspective, a smaller group is preferred, with three people as the ideal amount. As the number increases, the need for a facilitator is greater. The group members should be mindful of not monopolizing a discussion.

Key Tip: Stay engaged for the duration of the breakout session. Be aware of time without being ruled by it. Try not to be distracted by the notifications that indicate remaining time. Be aware of them, but don't let the notifications hinder or stop the flow of the discussion.

Zoom & Geography

You are anywhere.

With the proliferation of Zoom networking meetings and usage in countless groups, the notion of a group with a specific geographic location is no longer relevant. This changes the way we think about the physical location of a group.

For example, I lead a Provisors networking group in Downtown Los Angeles (DTLA) and live in Ventura, about 70 miles away. In a Zoom meeting, the DTLA designation is meaningless. Zoom and other such technologies are opening up previously limiting geographic barriers.

Zoom has truly broken down geographic limitations and allowed people to expand their networks wider than ever before.

Combatting Zoom Fatigue

There has been increasing attention to the phenomenon of Zoom Fatigue. It is real, though experienced differently by people. Constant gazing at the camera and other participants is demanding and tiring. We have to continually focus in a way not necessary in person.

Some people are self-conscious, and are pleased with the way they look on camera. It is preferable to be self-aware, to accept your appearance, and enhance it with proper hygiene, hairstyle, clothing attire, and make-up. Look as good as you can. YOU ARE YOUR BRAND!

Key Tips to Help with Zoom Fatigue

1. Take breaks if possible. Refrain from sitting and staring at a camera for long periods of time.

2. Hide yourself from your own view. If you don't want to stare at yourself for the duration of the meeting, and have full confidence in your appearance, this option may be great for you.

3. Don't overuse Zoom. You can always use other traditional channels such as phone, text or email.

4. Avoid multi-tasking or keep it to a minimum. Only multi-task when absolutely necessary.

5. Develop a plain (not too busy) background. This will help avoid over stimulation for others who have to look at you and your background.

SECTION 3 -
VIRTUAL NETWORKING

Making a Virtual Impact

Virtual networking requires some unique skills, especially as it relates to making an impact with new people. In-person meetings allowed face-to-face communication and the possible snippets of conversation with different people as we mingled and partook in some appetizers.

On Zoom, it can be more challenging to stand out and make an impact, particularly for introverts and guests. Use every possible means to present a positive impression, whether it be your background, introduction, or participation in breakout sessions. Stay engaged for the entire meeting and keep any chatting and multi-tasking to essential messages.

You might have to work harder and develop new skills in order to stand out, make connections, and further these connections with others.

Virtual Introductions (Elevator Speeches)

I have listened to thousands of introductions, known in the networking world as "elevator speeches." Some are great, some are okay, and some are dreadful and even cringeworthy.

The main goal of an introduction is for others to know your name, your company/firm, your main type of business, and what is a good referral for you.

Three Ingredients for a Memorable Introduction:

Clear

There should be no doubt about who you are and what you do, and this should be done in as few words as possible. It is important to time your introduction to make sure it meets the general guidelines and expectations. Speak clearly and loudly enough for others to hear you.

Concise

Less is More. Don't think that by saying more you will be remembered better. It is the impact, not the amount of words, that determines the effectiveness of an introduction. If you ramble on, you are likely to annoy or even repel people rather than attract them. Have respect for others' time and attention span.

Do you know how long 30 seconds is? Of course you do, but do you know it when you are speaking? Many people ramble on not to annoy others, but because they don't realize how long they have been speaking or simply don't know how to end their presentation. They might also be insensitive to others' reactions, which might include impatience and even annoyance.

I recommend that you time your introductions and testimonials to make sure that they are in accord with the time you are allotted. Remember that it doesn't take a long diatribe to make your point.

Catchy

Excellent introductions are memorable, and that is the most important aspect of them!

Say it, don't delay it. Conclude your introduction with some kind of tag line or "call me when". End them decisively.

You can either completely memorize your introduction, which is definitely preferable for beginners in networking. For more experienced or better known people, there can be more flexibility of exactly what you say and how you say it. Practice your introduction so that it flows naturally.

Virtual Troikas

Although troika is a specific term, this section could be applied to most small group interactions.

Networking groups often break people who attend the large meetings into groups (usually of 3 people) for a follow-up get together. The purpose of the smaller groups is to get to know others better in a small group setting.

The term troika (Russian for a group of three people working together) was used by some networking groups to designate the smaller group. Other groups use different names. Bruin Professionals, using the same concept, refers to the grouping as a Mini.

Smaller groups allow and encourage more interaction. Three is more preferable than four people in a group, as the smaller group allows for more discussion.

In the not too distant past, troikas would take place at a restaurant or some other meeting place. That was part of the deal. When you were placed in a troika with two (or three) others, you would all get your calendars, decide on breakfast, lunch, dinner, cocktails or some other meeting venue, and schedule the meeting.

Virtual troikas are a horse of a different color altogether. First of all, they don't need to conform to the traditional 60-90 minute meal or cocktail troika. Forty minutes is more of an ideal length and corresponds with the limit of non-paid Zoom accounts.

It is useful to have one member of the troika facilitate the conversation, especially for people who don't know each other or what others do for work. If the troika is composed of people who are already familiar with each other, a facilitator is less important.

I recommend that you make sure that everyone has ample opportunity to introduce themselves and their primary work focus, and then you can have a more free-floating conversation. Don't dominate the conversation. Be an attentive listener.

You could possibly show something of your work space. Virtual troikas take others literally into your world, so don't hesitate to show something personal in your Zoom Room. It could be a picture, a hobby or some other physical object.

One option is to have all members of a troika order the same type of food or food from the same restaurant.

Virtual happy hours are becoming increasingly popular and contribute to the feeling that we are relaxing and connecting in a more personal way with others. Since being outdoors is safer during the pandemic, outdoor troikas and socials can allow people to actually physically be closer to one another, as long as social distancing and masking are observed. If the outdoor space is large enough, the groups could be larger.

How do you end a troika? There is no simple answer to that, but the group needs to have some mechanism to terminate the troika. In some cases, everyone will naturally agree when to end the session. In other cases, there might be some members who want to continue the conversation, and one person who leaves the meeting sooner. There are no hard and fast rules for this, as our norms are still forming. I recommend that each group establish agreed upon parameters for ending a troika.

In addition to small group meetings of three or four, the one-on-one meeting is preferable overall. If you really want to get to know others in your organization or group, reach out to them and set up a one-on-one meeting. Be prepared for this meeting by learning something about the other person by looking up their LinkedIn profile. That way, you can build on what you already know rather than going into the meeting with no prior knowledge of the other person.

Virtual Happy Hours...Make Them Happy

In this age of social distancing, we miss seeing each other in person.

We have talked on the phone, emailed, texted and Zoomed. But we miss seeing each other face-to-face.

We can do that in a Happy Hour Zoom call. Schedule it late in the day when everyone can be fully engaged. Have your beverage and snack of preference within reaching distance. Your only limit should be common sense, because you don't have to drive after the meeting.

Have fun, connect, and let loose.

This is one of your best chances to stay connected.

If you are bolder, wear a mask, maintain social distance, and meet outdoors for similar effect. But in this option, two drink maximum.

Leading Virtual Networking Meetings: Requisite Skills

———

Leading virtual networking is similar in several ways to running an in-person meeting. You still need to have control of the meeting, adhere to time guidelines, have a plan and basic agenda, and review the things you intended to cover. You also need to show respect and pay attention to all attendees of the group. That should be your primary focus in running a meeting.

One major difference is the technical aspect of virtual meetings. It is important to have a tech monitor who assists with the technical "back stage". The monitor allows the Group Leader to focus on managing the meeting.

Currently, after six months of virtual meetings, there are a few aspects of Zoom that have proved as barriers to running a meeting. The most common one is the amount of chatting, both through the platform itself, or people texting, emailing, and doing other types of multi-tasking during the meeting. As a Group Leader, I have found much of that background activity to be distracting, just as I found people whispering to me during in-person meetings to be distracting.

One element of virtual leadership that is missing from in person is the ability to visually scan the room and to sense the "vibe" of the group. This is difficult to establish virtually. Some facilitation skills are transferable to Zoom, others are not. Virtual leaders need to learn new skills that can compensate for some of the limitations of virtual meetings.

The breakout rooms are quite useful and allow the leader to re-group when the breakout rooms are in operation. They can be used for introductions/elevator speeches, discussions, virtual mingling at the beginning of meetings, and to set up troikas or other future get-togethers at the end of meetings.

As the leader, you do need to pay some attention to the Chat in case something important is being directed to you. There is a danger of technical overload, which is different from leading an in-person meeting. Whereas an in-person leader can play off of the "crowd", the psychological dynamics are different in virtual meetings. You can't get someone's attention simply by eye contact or by intentional hesitation as you can face-to-face.

For me, the major adjustment in leading virtual meetings is the various inherent distractions in the virtual format like the Chat function. Another is the constant comings and goings of the attendees, which can be distracting and disorienting.

You should be clear about how you want attendees to use or not use Video. There should be some definite guidelines set by you regarding when it is acceptable or unacceptable to turn off your Video, muting/unmuting, re-naming, etc.

Challenges and Successes of Leading Zoom Networking Meetings

———

I have been leading, running and facilitating meetings and classes since 1972 with multiple topics, populations and sizes. I hadn't run a virtual meeting until spring of 2020. I knew right away that I didn't want to run the meeting AND operate the back end Zoom technology. I wanted to focus on running the meeting and staying 100% tuned in to the group. I would leave the technical end to someone else.

At first, I used my existing facilitation skills and my training and experience transferred to Zoom fairly well. I was immediately aware of the large amount of multi-tasking that was happening in these meetings. The Zoom platform seems to encourage a certain amount of it with the Chat function.

It was fundamentally different from running an in-person meeting, and in a few months, I became more comfortable with the platform and the technology. I liked the breakout rooms and consider them one of the best features of Zoom, especially for networking groups. What was missing from in-person meetings could be compensated for with breakout room interaction and discussions. I also like the polling option.

The groups I lead are experimenting with the timing, amount of participants and training for breakout room efficiency. Groups of four or fewer are ideal for breakout rooms. The amount of time allotted should vary depending on the topic and the length of the meeting.

Another thing we have learned is the advantage of putting attendees into breakout rooms shortly after the room is opened and prior to the start of the meeting. This is preferable to having a large group entering the room with one conversation. Those conversations can become awkward as more people enter the room, especially when a couple of people dominate the conversation.

Key Virtual Networking Tips

Networking is not only integral to success in business development, but it can also, and should, become a way of life. In order to derive success in networking, consider these steps for effective networking.

People have to first know you and what you do, like you, make some type of meaningful connection to you, and trust you based on knowing that you are excellent in your work before feeling comfortable enough to make a referral or introduction.

Likability is a MAJOR component of the networking process. People have to know your name, what you do, and be confident in your competency. But if they don't like you, then you won't get very far with them. People generally like others who are positive, fun to be around, and attentive listeners who are genuinely interested in them. It is important to pay attention to what others say and to build on prior conversations.

The following are the most fundamental networking tips that can be applied for both in-person and virtual networking:

1. **Show up consistently to meetings and troikas**. A sustained, focused effort is the key to success. Business networking is a form of marketing, and everything you do is part of that effort and strengthens your brand.

2. **Give to others.** Focus on what you can give without any expectation of getting anything in return. Pay it forward, and always think of new ways to be helpful to others. Ask others "How can I help you?" Give more than you receive. *Reciprocity* of some sort is preferred. It doesn't have to be strictly this for that, but you should have some loyalty to people who give things to you.

3. **Get involved in the groups where you are a member.** Volunteer, and whenever you do, follow up and do a good job. Whatever you do is a work sample and could lead to referrals. Reliability and dependability build trust. Always keep your commitments and follow up.

4. **Build relationships over time.** Include both business and personal conversations. Don't limit your conversations.

5. **Build your network wide and deep simultaneously.** Get to know others, what they do, and how you might work with them.

6. **Be a great listener.** Remember what others tell you about themselves. Bring up prior conversations to build on your relationships.

7. **Be yourself and be genuine.** People appreciate others who are real.

8. **Seek smaller groups.** This may be even more beneficial if you are more of an introvert. Reach out and set up a "virtual cup of coffee".

9. **Use whatever channel is offered, even if it isn't your preferred one.** For example, if someone strongly prefers a Zoom meeting or a phone call, be willing to respond accordingly.

10. **Always show respect to everyone.** Don't assume too much and maintain a positive attitude. Compliment others for good work that they have done. Don't complain, gossip or be critical of others publicly.

11. **Send thoughtful emails or texts to people in your network.** Do this without any motive or request for anything in return. Indicate that no response is needed, and that you just want to reconnect and check in with them.

12. **Ensure that your digital presence is up-to-date, accurate and relevant.** Clean up any mistakes so that your profile presents you in the best possible light.

13. **Continue to fine tune your introduction/elevator speech.** It should be crisp, clear and memorable.

14. **Follow up consistently with emails and social media communication.** You can use your own database to stay

in touch with your contacts, and to provide them with relevant information.

15. **Always maintain an attitude of gratitude.** Thank others for anything that they do on your behalf.

SECTION 4 -
PSYCHOLOGY

Psychological Concepts/Skills for Networking

There are a number of key psychological concepts and skills that make an effective networker. First and foremost is an attitude of giving. You should approach networking with the notion of what you can give to others in terms of making introductions (being a connector), referrals, and offering trusted advice when asked. Be a giver, and you will receive in return.

Be a good listener! If you listen to others attentively with complete focus and with genuine curiosity, people will share their stories more willingly, and they will like you. Strong and consistent listening skills will lead to many mutually beneficial relationships. It is important not only to listen carefully, but also to remember what they tell you about themselves so that you can build on that information in future conversations.

As you listen, empathy is an important characteristic that will assist you in seeing others' situation and point of view. Empathy is the ability to accurately understand and in some way, identify with the world of others and what they are facing in their lives. Counselors depend on this skill, and it makes sense for us to develop it. As you listen and remember what others tell you about their work and life, do so without interrupting, judging or being in a hurry to talk about yourself. As you hear things that require empathic responses, communicate your understanding and confirm that you are on the correct wavelength. Empathy is an effective tool in problem solving. "I know you must be upset about this situation, and I will do everything I can to solve it" is an effective response, and much appreciated by others. Focus more on others and less on yourself.

Be genuine and sincere. Tell the truth. Don't hesitate to share your true feelings. People respond to real people, not phony people. If you want to build strong and enduring relationships, get into the personal realm. It is expected to talk business and ask business questions like "How is your work?", but those types of discussions don't really do much to build any type of deep relationships.

Conversations should have a balance between business and personal conversations. There are many options in terms of which comes first, and every situation is a bit different.

Circadian Rhythms: Time and Networking

What time is good for you?

Actually, what time is best for you?

Recently my son asked if we could do a call at 12 noon. I declined, in all honesty, because that is my nap time. Yup, I said it without shame or remorse.

Everyone has their own unique circadian rhythms, which means that they have peak and valley times over 24 hours.

For example, my friend George goes to bed at 8 p.m. and awakes at 3 a.m.

My friend Leslie goes to bed at 5 a.m. and wakes up at 12 noon (or later).

They have quite opposite biorhythms.

We all have tendencies that we typically prefer.

The most common and well known are the early bird (or lark) and night owl.

These tendencies affect our choice in times of networking meetings. For example, some people hate early morning meetings while others prefer them. Personally, I dislike noon meetings because of my preference for a rest at that time. I prefer early morning meetings, the earlier the better.

What is your preferred and most productive time of day?

Whatever it is (there is no right or wrong here), you should devote your most important work to that time. I like to write (important to me) at my peak times, which are both early morning and late afternoon.

Another aspect of time that is critical to planning your networking activities is how much time you have to devote to business and personal networking. Depending on your answer, this should influence how many networking meetings you attend and how much time you spend on such things as social media posting and communication.

A number of years ago, I did some networking training with associates at a large, national law firm. They were a young, bright and highly motivated group. But they had been instructed by the partners in their firm to bill as many hours as possible. Thus, they only had very limited time for networking and needed to be very strategic in what networking group(s) they joined and participated in. It was a real dilemma for the aspiring associates who hoped to become partners one day. Bill as many hours as possible, but also bring in new clients or you won't make partner. This dual message makes it quite challenging for these attorneys who are striving to make partner status in the firm.

Professionals who are primarily in business development and don't have to actually perform the work can and should spend more time networking. They should likely join more than one group and guest at other groups within their networking organization if possible.

In addition, the amount of time you have to network and the geographic range of possible clients will determine how wide and deep you build your network. If you have unlimited time, you should definitely go as wide and deep as possible, especially if you can secure business in any region.

If your time is more like those attorney associates, it is preferable to select fewer groups and meetings and go deep within those groups.

During the pandemic, many people have more time, and that is one reason that the networking meetings are currently so packed. Well, the rooms aren't packed, just the screens.

There can be an enormous time savings with virtual networking meetings. Many people are commenting on how much easier it is overall to attend a Zoom meeting vs. in person.

I had a troika recently with Teddy and Marijane. They are both frequent attendees of Zoom meetings for Bruin Professionals, yet were adamant about how in-person meetings were more difficult to attend due to geographic reasons.

Going forward, networking groups need to consider the positive experiences people have been having with Zoom and other technologies, and perhaps rethink the previous model which was location and in-person driven.

Time and Networking

How much time should you spend networking?

The answer depends primarily on the nature of your business and the amount of time you have in your schedule.

If you primarily do business development, then you will likely spend a lot of time networking, whether in person (when we are able to that that again) or virtually.

It's not how much time you have, but how you use your time that matters.

Are you spending enough quality time networking?

Now is the time to build your virtual network as much as possible and hopefully you have the time to do it!

Key Tips to Maximize Time

1. Be strategic. Attend groups meetings and events that are relevant to your work.

2. Decide how to build your network. Is it more beneficial for you to increase your network wide or deep (or both)?

3. Stay in the moment. Learn as much as you possibly can about people in your groups.

4. Schedule specific times for phone calls. If you do call someone without a time slot, always ask at the beginning, "Is this a good time to talk?"

5. Plan and monitor your various networking activities. Use a calendar or spreadsheet and be strategic and thoughtful in your time management.

The Influence of Age and Stage

O ur involvement in networking is largely influenced by our age and stage in our career. Older, more established professionals might consider the pros and cons of virtual networking and decide to dial things back a bit in terms of their attendance. Depending on the stage of your business career, personal, and financial life, you will have a varied relationship with networking.

As a 70 something with a long career behind me, my networking needs and requirements are quite different from a younger, less experienced person. Everyone has a different level of experience and need for new clients. It is important to take longevity (or lack thereof) into account in determining how to approach different aspects of the networking process, what you do, and when you do it.

There can be a marked difference in networking styles depending on how well and how long you have known people. When people know exactly who you are and what you do, then you can move into deeper and different levels of communication.

I have observed that networking veterans who have been in a group for a long time and have established relationships often use social events to deepen those relationships, rather than focusing on meeting new people. Less experienced people or those new to networking, however, are more likely to meet as many people as possible, and need to explain who they are and what they do.

Versatility and Relationships

Are you basically the same with everyone you meet and know?

If so, you are limiting the scope and breadth of relationships. In order to be successful in building mutually beneficial relationships with a wide variety of people, you need to be versatile in how you relate to others.

What does this mean?

Essentially, it means not saying and doing the same things with everyone you meet. What you talk about, how you talk about it, how long you talk about it, and what you find meaningful will differ for each person you meet. Thus, it is preferable to have a wide range of topics that you are able to discuss with others.

Take humor for example (Ha Ha, LOL). I have noticed that humor is not only the common ingredient in ALL of my close friendships, but that each friend and I find different things funny. For example, I've known my friend Paul Bunce for 55 years and we share humor that is very specific to our mutual experiences. No one else would think our conversations are the least bit funny. We still find humor in the events that occurred and the people we met when we worked together as teenagers at McDonald's in Pasadena. FYI, hamburgers were 18 cents and fries were 15 cents.

My buddy Danny Lyman and I share very unique humor about our experiences in American Samoa that is funny to us and certainly no one else.

The true joy of relationships (for me at least) stems from the various types of experiences and interactions.

As you learn about people and what they are truly interested in, you should remember the unique conversations and try not to discuss the same things with everyone. Don't be a one trick pony!

Pay close attention to what others talk about and their interests. Search for common ground with each person you meet.

Why is this important? In order to build a diverse network, you need to be versatile in what you talk about, and not tell the same stories to everyone. Some might be quite interested, while others have completely different interests and senses of humor.

Vary your routine, and forge different relationships with different people.

Humor - Ya gotta laugh

H umor is one of the most important ingredients in many strong relationships. We like to laugh. It relaxes us, makes us feel better, and brings us real, positive emotions.

Humor is very important to me. I love to laugh and like to make other people laugh. I did stand up comedy in the 80s, somewhat unsuccessfully, but I did it. All of my close friendships have humor (unique with each friendship) at the core.

Years ago, I had a troika with two other people, one an attorney and the other a financial advisor named Gary. I had already met over one hundred financial advisors, had my own advisor, and would likely run into several new ones soon. I was cordial with Gary, but told him that it was unlikely I would make a referral to him. He wasn't actively soliciting my business, but I was really just making a statement about how many advisors I already knew.

Gary was very funny and did some impressive and hilarious impressions. It was refreshing for me not to hear about stock market. It was a fun troika, and I was struck with Gary's humor.

That same night I was giving a presentation to a group about networking. I commented on how funny the guy was at lunch. A woman immediately raised her hand and asked if I could refer Gary, the funny financial advisor. I made the referral to Gary the next day.

By his unique brand of being funny, Gary received a referral. I am not sure if he got the business, but it gave me a story. The big takeaway is that many people like to be around others who are funny.

Humor really is a great way to enhance relationships. I'm not talking about off-color, racist or sexist jokes. But finding a common humorous ground can yield some wonderful relationships. Humor is more difficult to utilize on Zoom due primarily to the challenge of not hearing responses.

If you want to better gauge people's responses, you should look for any facial or body language to indicate their response (or lack thereof) to your presentation. If you are doing something intended to be humorous, you could ask everyone to unmute themselves so you can hear their bellowing laughter.

The Dangers of Stereotypes

In order to make sense out of the world, people tend to stereotype others based on common tendencies often found by members of that particular group. These stereotypes might represent positive, negative, or neutral characteristics believed to be common for a group.

Stereotypes can be used for age, ethnicity, religion or political persuasion.

The danger of stereotypes is that they are just generalizations and not true in all cases. Sometimes stereotypes can help keep us safe, like assuming that someone with a gun demanding our money is dangerous, or that a barking pit bull we don't know rushing towards us could be problematic.

Common stereotypes

Accountants tend to be introverts.

Lawyers are argumentative.

Bankers are gifted in math.

However, it is important to be cautious in your use of stereotypes. Don't let them determine your reaction to everyone in that category. The more people you know of any group, the more you realize the diversity that exists among that group.

For example, while it is true that some attorneys are contentious and litigious, some are very agreeable and gentle.

We all know the dangers of negative stereotypes, as they have led to some of the worst atrocities in history. There are also positive stereotypes, like assuming Asians are good in math, which might be unfair to the Asian person who is not.

Be aware of the various ways in which your biases, preconceptions and stereotypes might be inaccurate and in need of adjustment.

Self-Perception and the Perception of Others

We see ourselves in a certain way. We could perceive and label ourselves as smart, friendly, shy, old, young, tall, or thin. The list goes on and on. Others may perceive us quite differently, and we may or may not learn about their varied perceptions.

In social interactions, this variation from self-perception and the perceptions of others can influence how people make decisions and relate to one another. People might think that someone is intimidating and unapproachable, and yet that person perceives himself as open and approachable. The truth often lies somewhere in between.

Bob might perceive himself as shy, while others could perceive him as stuck up. It is useful to find out how others perceive you, and whether it matches or is in conflict with your self-perception. Candid conversations can help elucidate and clarify these discrepancies.

Pay attention to these stated perceptions about you. If you feel that they are incorrect or unfair characterizations, don't hesitate to have a conversation to have them adjusted or modified.

Key Tip: There is a useful tool to make sure that your perceptions are accurate, referred to as the Perception Check. When you are uncertain about your perception of a person, their feelings or behavior, ask them as a way of checking the validity of your perceptions. It could go something like this: "I noticed that you seemed to be upset. Are you upset, or is something else going on?"

Roles and Their Influence

We all play various roles in our lives. For example, a person can have the roles of:

Family	Leadership	Participant
• Mother	• Boss	• Employee
• Father	• Group Leader	• Group Member
• Son	• Uber Driver	• Uber Rider
• Daughter	• Teacher	• Student
• Brother	• Performer	• Audience Member
• Sister	• Clergy	• Parishioner
	• Coach	• Player
	• Referee	

There are times when these roles might conflict with one another. For example, you might be the coach of a team when one of the players is your son. You might be President of an organization that your boss joins and have to determine who's the boss in the new situation.

I work with my son Billy. He is still my son, but in a work setting, our roles change in a number of ways depending upon the exact situation. We could be preparing a presentation, ordering food in a restaurant, talking of his career or mine, or playing baseball with his son (my grandson).

Roles can create confusing and sometimes uncomfortable dilemmas. Understanding the numerous roles that you play, and the roles of others in your sphere, can greatly assist you in nurturing mutually beneficial relationships with others.

Another dimension directly related to this is *dual relationships.* The best example of this is the danger of establishing a personal friendship with your boss (or vice versa). It can work, but the potential for conflict is quite real. In general, dual relationships like this have potential pitfalls and should be carefully considered and discussed prior to pursuing them.

It is important to have clear *boundaries,* such as who you invite into your home or who you give your bank password to (NO ONE!). Psychotherapists, for example must have very clear and strict boundaries with their patients (e.g. not dating or going on vacations with them).

Some people have strict boundaries in terms of networking. They keep things 100% business (a mistake), and clearly differentiate between their business network and their friendships. There are pros and cons to this issue. My opinion is that you need to be prudent, but there are definite benefits and joys to developing friendships, and you never know where you will find them.

Another aspect of these dimensions is *status,* perceived or real. Someone might have very high status in one of their roles (like group leader) and low status in

94

another (new member). It is preferable to treat everyone with respect, regardless of their status. Status can be measured by age, experience, net worth or other factors.

Primacy and Recency: Serial Position Effect

There is an interesting psychological concept about when we hear or see something and the effect that sequence has on our memory. Research has found that we tend to remember the first and last in a series of things or information we are presented.

The material in the middle is remembered less well. This is referred to as the serial position effect. Primacy refers to the first things in a series, and recency the last.

Therefore, when you are introducing yourself or making a point, place an emphasis on the first and last things you say.

This effect explains why advertisements often give the phone number or web site at the end (and often repeat it incessantly).

It is useful to practice and revise your introduction. Work on having a powerful beginning and ending, as they will be remembered most of anything you say. Unique tag lines tend to stick with people, and you should develop one that is memorable and catchy.

Primacy and recency also applies to people you meet and have met. We tend to remember the people we have met most recently, and often forget those we haven't seen in awhile. Therefore, it is quite useful to reach out to people from the past.

Freeing and Binding Questions: Toward Better Communication

When we are in a conversation with others, the types of questions we ask can largely determine to nature and flow of the conversation. There are two types of questions that you can ask:

Freeing Questions

Open-ended questions that allow others to elaborate, e.g. "What are some things you liked about your vacation?" or "Tell me about your vacation."

Binding Questions

Close-ended (Yes/No) questions that don't allow for much response, e.g. "Did you have fun?"

Freeing responses are much more preferable, especially when your intention is to get others to express themselves.

Pay attention to the type of questions you ask people when you meet them. Use more open-ended questions that free others to elaborate and expand on your conversations.

Besides, if you only ask Yes/No questions, you will have to keep asking them because their answers will all be brief.

Report Talk and Rapport Talk

It has been stated that in general, some people tend to engage more commonly in "report talk", focusing on events, facts and things other than personal feelings. They might talk about sports scores, hobbies or projects they are working on, but rarely about any personal topics or feelings related to them.

On the other hand, others are more likely to talk about feelings and showing empathy for others with whom they are talking. This is referred to as "rapport talk".

In order to truly build relationships, it is useful to engage more in the second type of conversation. This can be done in response to personal comments made by others. Another way is for you to bring up personal topics when appropriate.

In order to truly establish a strong and lasting rapport with others, you need to get beyond "small talk" like the weather, sports and traffic. Report talk can be used as the starting point in a conversation, but in order to build deeper relationships, get personal about yourself and respond fully when others do so in order to build and nurture true and enduring rapport with others.

NETWORKING IN THE VIRTUAL AGE

Self-Disclosure

S elf-disclosure occurs when we share something personal, and possibly something which makes us vulnerable about ourselves. It can occur among friends or in networking. There is tremendous potential value in self-disclosure. It makes us more human and allows others to see our fuller self.

Though you need to be prudent in what you share and when you share it, that sharing allows others to become closer to you. Deep and abiding relationships usually involve a certain amount of personal revelation.

Your degree of self-disclosure should always be guided by appropriateness! You need to determine how much to disclose and when to disclose it.

Pay careful attention to others. When they disclose something personal about themselves, respond with understanding and empathy when possible. Encourage them to talk about things that are important to them. Remember these conversations in order to build deeper relationships over time which go beyond superficial topics.

Introversion and Extroversion

The introversion/extroversion factor is critically important in virtual networking. In person, introverts tend to be shy, less talkative and not totally comfortable in a large group meeting. There are degrees of introversion. Extroverts are more gregarious and often talkative people. There are also ranges of extroversion, as well as situations in which people tend to be more introverted or extroverted.

In virtual networking, it is likely that the extrovert will still be more outgoing than timid. The introvert might feel even shyer on Zoom, but find a way to express themselves, possibly with the Chat function.

Some people who are quiet in a large crowd might be able to feel more outgoing in a virtual format. There is a significant difference in speaking in front of a live group and talking via Zoom.

Factors that can influence our attitudes and behavior in person might have less or no impact virtually. For example, attire, make-up, shoes, physical size and psychological comfort levels can affect how much we enjoy public events (or dread them).

In general, extroverts are likely to be less affected by the varying formats than introverts. This virtual world could be the opportunity for quieter people to shine and not be overshadowed by the more outgoing and garrulous extroverts.

Nexus Concept

The nexus concept explains a lot about human interaction. The nexus is the central, integral member of a group of people and is usually the center of influence in a group. For example, if Jill introduces Sue to Barbara, and knows both of them better than they know each other, Jill would be the nexus. Sue and Barbara don't seek each other out without Jill and rely on Jill to initiate any interaction among them.

The leader of a group is often the nexus, or a nexus among the members. They attend every meeting, know everyone in the group, and might help organize any additional get togethers.

When joining a new group, it is useful to get to know who the nexus is, to meet them, and get them to know and like you. By meeting and building a positive and strong relationship with the nexus of the group, you will become assimilated into the group much more quickly.

In addition to determining who is the nexus of a group, you can actually become the nexus over time by being deeply involved in a group. When you do that, your influence within a group becomes much more substantial. Embrace the power that comes with being the nexus while always remaining humble.

Group Dynamics

When a networking group meets in person, there is a different, tangible group dynamic that happens as the group assembles and during the meeting itself. It is a bit different every time a particular group meets, and part of the value of meeting in person.

No such group dynamics are present in Zoom meetings. You join from your home or office, usually alone.

The group dynamics prior to the in-person meeting include the informal conversations and mingling as people approach and talk to various others as well as getting to know them and what they are doing. We can introduce people who might not already know each other.

It is this experience that people are missing in virtual networking, the palpable feeling and joy of actually physically connecting with others.

Some people enjoy this part of the meeting the most, and might even wish it lasted longer than the normal 15 to 30 minutes (depending on the group).

In order to mitigate the effects of not meeting in person, one-on-one virtual meet ups are strongly suggested. Rather than lamenting the effects of social distancing, embrace the various channels of virtual communication, and continue to connect with others.

Conformity: Impact on Group Behavior

People conform to the majority in many cases and in many different ways. Conformity was studied heavily by psychologists because of its prevalence. The most cited early research was that of Solomon Asch.

Asch brought the subjects into a room with a group of experimental accomplices, who gave knowingly incorrect answer to a visual perception experiment. The subjects were shown two lines that were obviously different lengths, and the majority of the accomplices asserted that they were all the same length. The subjects concurred with the majority despite their visual perceptions.

Thus, people were willing to ignore their perception of reality and give incorrect answers in order to conform to the majority. The application to networking is the degree to which people conform to norms of attire, giving introductions, where to place the name tag, and how to give a correct testimonial.

Every group engenders a certain amount of conformity. As virtual networking increases, this can be seen in how groups develop norms of behavior and how members of the groups conform to them. An example of conformity is how people agree to and conform to the various aspects of virtual etiquette as they are established.

Networking Norms

I first learned about social norms as an undergraduate Psychology student at UCLA. The concept was and still is quite interesting to me. Every group develops a set of norms that are learned and followed by the majority (in some cases the vast majority) of people in that group.

Things like drinking, smoking cigars, wearing short pants, wearing hats, eating meat, and the list goes on, are tolerated or even encouraged in some groups and forbidden in others.

Networking groups are no different. Norms are set and have been set in each different networking group. But some of the norms for in-person meetings no longer apply in this virtual world like dressing in business attire and wearing name tags.

New norms, sometimes referred to as etiquette, are forming. This section will address some of the most prominent norms that are emerging. Keep in mind that some norms are pretty firm and agreed upon by most people. There are other norms that are more fluid and open to opinion. My interviews and discussions have shown that there is a wide range of opinion on such things as frequency of using the Chat function or Video function.

Norms will be established by networking groups and chapters within those groups. Some group leaders will want people to follow strict rules, while others will point out major norms like knowing how to quickly unmute and mute yourself and not going before the camera undressed.

The development of any type of norms is dependent upon conformity to expected attitudes and behavior. Dressing a certain way becomes a norm (whatever it is) because the majority of people conform to that expectation. For example, it is a norm in most business meetings that men do not wear hats into the meeting. Of course there are variations of that norm. In fact, some people actually try to differentiate themselves by wearing a hat when no one else in a particular group does so.

In large virtual networking meetings, it is the norm for most participants to be muted. Most people conform to that norm. There is often a learning curve, wherein it takes awhile for some people to learn behavior that is commonly accepted and adhered to by the majority of the participants.

Strengths Perspective: Application to Networking

As stated in my dedication, Dennis Saleebey (my cousin) pioneered a theory of social work in his tenure at University of Kansas called the Strengths Perspective. It basically stated that the best way for people to grow and develop was to focus on their strengths and build from there. We are all good or highly skilled in some areas, and we need to determine what they are and how to build on them.

This perspective has a direct application to networking. Be yourself, and use your existing strengths to be the best networker you can be.

Whether your strengths are speaking, listening, empathy, humor or anything else, become aware of them and use them to your advantage. If you are more of an introvert, you can focus on your strong listening skills rather than bemoaning your shyness.

Focus on your strong points, develop them, and use them to build mutually beneficial relationships.

SECTION 5 -
NETWORKING BASICS

Wide/Deep Networking Revisited: What Has Changed

When I wrote my other two networking books (*Connecting: Beyond the Name Tag and Connecting: Key Networking Tips for Business and Life*), I discussed the various advantages to taking your network wide and/or deep.

In general, you would go wide if you had more time, did business in wider regions, and wanted a large, diverse network.

You would go deep when you had less time to network, your fewer groups had all the resources you need, and your choice was a smaller, more intimate network.

If you have any interest in taking your network wide, NOW IS THE TIME. As long as networking groups are not placing limitations on how many times you can guest at a group, take it wide. There is such thing as overexposure, and that does need to be considered.

However, just because you can go anywhere doesn't mean that is the best strategy. If you are going to different geographic regions, have something to offer when you do so. Don't just go for the novelty or because you can. As in all networking decisions, consider what you have to offer and what are the possible benefits to you. In general, there is minimal value in merely attending a lot of meetings because you can. That is going wide without going deep or building truly meaningful and mutually valuable relationships.

Testimonials and the Role of Gratitude in Networking

Testimonials are an integral component of the networking process. It is vital to properly thank others publicly (and privately) for introductions, referrals and work they have performed for you or your clients. The testimonial should be more about the person you are thanking than about you.

Your testimonial should say a bit about the other person and their work, and it serves as a secondary introduction of them. Be mindful about any things done by others for you, and thank them in a timely manner. Make sure you learn and remember some important facts about them to make a proper testimonial.

If you have enough time in your testimonial, briefly describe the nature of the transaction if it is not confidential or privileged information. By doing so, attendees might be reminded about others' work and how they might make an introduction or referral to them.

Get Involved

———

Participation in your group is vital to success in networking. The most successful networkers get involved, volunteer for projects, and follow through with things they commit to doing. Keep in mind that everything you do (or don't do) in a group is a *work sample*. People will judge you by how well you perform.

Do what you say you are going to do when you say you are going to do it. Your competence will go a long way toward getting people to trust you and do business with you. One of the best ways to rise to the top of your group is to show up, raise your hand to volunteer, and do your part to the very best of your ability.

If You Don't Schmooze, You Lose

I was interviewing a Provisors Group Leader, Ivy Rappaport, and asked her what she misses about in-person meetings.

Without any hesitation, she said, "There is no schmoozing." Schmoozing, which happens before the meeting actually starts, allows people to chat informally, catch up and joke around. Several people have indicated that it is their favorite part of the meeting.

This informal segment, free-floating and casual, is quite useful in getting people to shake hands, build relationships and enjoy a cup of coffee and food.

On the other hand, virtual meetings put us in a square next to others in a random (not chosen) manner.

The informal schmoozing is especially important to new members, where introductions can take place and you can have snippets of conversations which are unlikely to occur at virtual meetings.

Much of the relationship building that happens prior to or after the meeting is an indispensable part of an in-person meeting.

There are some viable ways to somewhat replicate schmoozing over Zoom. The best way is a one-on-one Zoom call or a troika. Especially among people who already know each other, schmoozing is possible in small groups.

Relationship Building in One-on-One Meetings

Networking does not mean you need to be in a large group. In fact, some of the best conversations happen in a one-on-one setting. You're able to dive much deeper when you can connect with someone individually than if you are in a group. In order to maximize the interaction, here are some suggestions.

Make it about them, not you. It's easy to fall into the trap of talking about yourself, but be careful to not dominate the conversation. Remember that people love to talk about themselves so it's important to be great at asking questions. The more you learn about the person you're meeting, the more it will help you understand what they are all about. Ask questions about their business, but it's also valuable to ask personal questions to get to know them as a human being. Are they married, do they have kids, where did they go to school, what do they like to do in their free time? What are they passionate about and what are their hobbies or interests? The more you know about the other person, the easier it will be for you to connect with them. Relationships are about finding common ground, so the more possibilities you have to find that common ground, the greater connection you will build with that person.

You don't want to exclusively ask questions without giving any information about yourself. Ideally, a one-on-one meeting should allow for a back-and-forth conversation where you both freely share information about each other in a casual and conversational way.

If it is an initial one-on-one meeting, meaning you've never met before or don't really know each other very well, then you could spend part of the meeting allowing them to introduce themselves and another part of the meeting sharing your story.

Another important thing to remember is to understand how you can help and support the person you're meeting with. Having a clear idea of what they do will allow you to make some assumptions of how you can best provide value to that person. But don't rely on your assumptions alone! Actually ask what is the best way for you to support or help them. This will help to create even greater clarity around what the person is looking for. You may think they are looking for new clients when in reality they actually may want something entirely different.

Engage with them in a friendly way throughout the conversation and remember some of the fundamentals of communication like smiling throughout, infusing humor, making a great first impression, maintaining eye contact, and being genuinely curious about them throughout your one-on-one meeting.

Remember that the one-on-one session is an opportunity for you to connect on a deeper level. Go two, three, or four levels deep by asking follow-up questions and allowing their story to be more intimately shared beyond the surface.

SECTION 6 -
CASE STUDIES

The following case studies are real-life examples of the various ways in which people are responding and adapting to social distancing. They reflect some of the diverse reactions that people are having to virtual communication.

Case Study - Mike the Lawyer

———

Mike is a 35 year old attorney in a medium-sized law firm. He has been in a networking group (Provisors) for two years. I had a troika with him recently, and asked him how he likes Zoom networking meetings vs. in-person meetings. He was clear in his answer. He strongly preferred and wants to return to in-person meetings.

Upon me asking why, he indicated that he really likes the face-to face conversations prior to the meetings and didn't like the inability to get a verbal audience response on Zoom. He didn't feel he came across strongly on Zoom, and he missed the responses (laughter, facial expressions) that were common at in-person meetings. He is slowly adapting to large group Zoom networking meetings, but he doesn't like them.

He likes the breakout rooms because they are more of a small group and unmuted discussion. He also enjoys virtual troikas, again because of the small group interaction.

Given the unlikelihood of returning to the board room any time soon, Mike would be well-advised to improve his existing skills and strengths with virtual meetings. He could schedule one-on-one meetings with fellow members of his group. Additionally, he needs to accept the lack of reactions rather than waiting for them.

Case Study - Zelda the Zoomer

Zelda is a 65 year old banker. She is well established in her career and is not really looking for new business. She lives about 45 minutes from her monthly, early morning networking meeting in Downtown Los Angeles. She has been in her group for fifteen years. For Zelda, Zoom meetings are a welcome respite from waking up very early, getting ready, driving to the meeting, finding parking and going through security.

She likes her group very much, but hates the work it takes to get there. I queried her about virtual vs. in-person meetings, and she indicated that she would be quite happy if she never had to attend an in-person morning meeting again. However, she would be eager to attend socially distanced outdoor social events.

Her networking group has become more of a social gathering and a way to meet possible sources for her to refer. Zelda still attends every meeting of her group and indicated that she doesn't miss much from the in-person meetings.

Case Study - Bob the Group Leader

Bob leads a Provisors networking group. I interviewed him about his experience using Zoom to run his meetings. He indicated that he was having difficulty tracking and remembering the comments made by people during the meeting. He had "tricks" to remember people and comments during in-person meetings, which he can't really use on Zoom.

He mentioned that in a room you hear everything, but on Zoom you could only really hear what was being said by the speaker.

Bob is a dynamic group leader who likes leading an in-person group much like a band conductor. He enjoys the back-and-forth conversation in person that is simply not the same in virtual meetings.

One thing Bob has done is set up and facilitate Virtual Happy Hours for his group. Everyone is unmuted during those sessions, which allows Bob to have the back-and-forth that he so enjoys about in-person meetings.

Case Study - Justin the Newbie

———

Justin is a 32 year old accountant, relatively new to networking and networking groups. He expressed his opinion about the difficulty of "tailoring" or modifying a conversation like we can do face-to-face. He stated that he thinks Zoom is good for maintaining existing long term relationships, but less so for developing new ones due to the limited facial and body language.

He lamented that it is difficult to gauge people's reactions to what is being said. As he was giving a presentation and sharing his screen, he had to scroll to discern people's reaction to what he was saying. Not having immediate visual and auditory reactions and feedback made it more challenging to present.

I suggested that Justin query a few members of his group to assess their reactions to his presentation and how he comes across on Zoom, rather than merely assuming their reactions.

Case Study - Nancy the Hugger

N ancy, who owns her own insurance agency, misses the in-person meetings very much.

"I miss you guys. I'm a hugger."

There is a tangible, palpable difference when you are face-to-face with people you really like.

Nancy went on to explain the real affection she has for her "home" group, and the value that she gets from attending the meetings in person.

She mentioned "Zoom Fatigue" and that she strongly preferred the in-person meetings over the virtual ones, despite the absence of long drives in traffic, putting on make-up and getting dressed in business attire.

After speaking at length with Nancy, it occurred to me that Nancy has *warmth*, and people with warm and affectionate personalities tend to love people and enjoy being around others in person.

Warmth is a characteristic that few people would use to describe themselves, but accounts for a lot in the likability dimension. The opposite of warmth is coldness, and few people would argue that coldness is an admirable characteristic.

Case Study - Phil the Extrovert Techie

Phil is a new member of a networking group and has never attended an in-person networking meeting. He is quite positive about Zoom, and explained that he has been using Zoom for many years and feels extremely comfortable with the technology and various features associated with it.

In addition, he describes himself as an extrovert. He feels that the combination of knowing the technology and his extroversion are the main reasons he has been able to forge new relationships without any face-to-face contact.

For people new to networking who are entering it in a virtual world, two things are useful. First, learn and become comfortable with the many features of Zoom. Secondly, try to speak clearly and forcibly during meetings, even if you are more of an introvert.

SECTION 7 -
KEY
QUESTIONS

What's Your Goal?

When I first started in networking, my goal was simple and clear. I wanted to have more business referred to me. I hadn't heard about the Pay it Forward idea or being a giver. That came later as I learned.

At first, I thought the idea was to meet as many people and get as many business cards as possible. That was lots of breadth with no depth. This was before social media, and even before email and texting.

Now my goal is much less about getting business than nurturing and enjoying the friendships of the relationships I have cultivated over many years. If you are newer to networking and your job is business development, I recommend a combination of making new relationships and developing the ones you have.

Your networking program should be tailored to your current and possible future goals. The following questions are all related to integral aspects of the our current situation. Consider each of them carefully, and answer the questions. There are no right or wrong answers.

> **Why are you in a networking group anyway?**
>
> **What are your goals?**
>
> **Are you looking to expand your sphere of influence?**
>
> **Are you looking to expand your business?**
>
> **Are you looking to find sources to refer business?**
>
> **Are you looking for friendship?**

Depending on what you are trying to accomplish, you will approach networking in a particular way.

Do We Need to Meet in Person?

When all is said and done (at least for now) about virtual vs. in-person meetings, the question remains:

DO WE NEED TO MEET IN PERSON?

We may not need to, because we have survived over six months of not doing so.

Of course it is better, and there are many reasons to meet face-to-face. There is a discernible difference to meeting in person, shaking hands (when we did that), observing body language, and displaying it.

In sales, for example, meeting in person has always been perceived as a preferred strategy to phone calls or sending information electronically. This is especially true when selling high dollar goods or services.

In person, you have the potential to experience more senses like touch, feel and smell. You can also see movement and other mannerisms that are not present in virtual communication. There is a definite benefit to meeting in person!

However, there are many times that we don't need to meet that we met prior to the pandemic, like for signing paperwork or doing a physical inventory when it could be transacted electronically.

So when should we meet, and when should we use virtual channels? Some examples are obvious, like getting together with family and friends as well as valued business associates. We might just want to get together with people we like.

The bottom line is that there are definitely clear advantages to meeting in person. In the future, we need to be flexible, use virtual communication when there is no physical contact allowed, and reflect on when we should use each channel.

How Important is Convenience?

———————

Many people have commented how much more convenient virtual meetings are, compared to in-person meetings. How important is the convenience factor in determining your preference for virtual or in-person meetings?

Does the convenience outweigh the limitations of virtual meetings?

Do any limitations of virtual meetings outweigh any convenience factor?

What would we do differently if most future meetings were virtual? Would we adapt or somehow find in-person networking meetings?

Some people believe that any limitations of virtual meetings are outweighed by the various conveniences, while others favor the convenience factor and believe that virtual meetings can provide enough of the essential benefits needed for effective networking and business development.

What is your opinion on this matter?

The Organization or the Person?

Some people join networking organizations and become zealots of that organization. The organization becomes primary, and the "true believers" are extremely loyal to the organization. They sometimes become life members, whether it be Rotary, Provisors, BNI or Elks Club.

That is expected, and there is nothing wrong with that approach.

For others, it is the people with whom they develop relationships that are the central focus. So they might join a networking group, stay in it for five years, and then decide for some reason to drop out of the group.

The relationships they build are theirs, not the organization's. They can and should keep the relationships. They don't end when the person leaves the organization and can endure indefinitely as long as they are maintained and nourished by calls or lunches.

In my opinion, it is the person, not the organization, that is the important thing. Maintain the relationships and stay in touch.

How about you?

Are you more attached to the organization or the people in it?

How Important is that Call?

As we are navigating the world of Zoom and Zoom Etiquette, the question arises about when to take a call during a networking meeting. One view is that when you are in a networking meeting, that should be your primary focus and only a true emergency would be a sufficient reason to take a phone call. I was talking with an attorney named Al, and he stated that he would always take a client call during a networking meeting. I asked him if he would do the same thing at an in-person meeting. He declined to answer.

As stated previously, multi-tasking during Zoom networking meetings has become a real issue, and there is no consensus about the proper decorum. My position is that when you are in a meeting, even a Zoom meeting, that should be your focus. Your phone should be on silent, and your full attention should be on the virtual meeting. The real questions are:

How important is that call?

Can't you just wait, let the person leave a message, and call them back immediately after the meeting?

Common courtesy dictates that it is better to stay focused on the meeting you are in, rather than allowing yourself to be interrupted by another call. There are emergencies and reasons to take the call, but that should not be done in most cases.

What Channel Are You On?

Because of the pandemic, Zoom has been a popular "channel" to continue networking. People tend to have their channel preferences, that is, the way they prefer to communicate with others.

Basic Channels		
Meeting in person	Telephone	Text
Email	Social Media - Many options and variations	Zoom, Teams or Webex
Electronic News-letters	Hard Copy News-letters	Handwritten Letters

Zoom has become exceedingly popular lately, and sometimes people opt for Zoom calls when they could just use the phone. It is a current fad, and I'm not sure how long it will remain in vogue. Some people limit themselves to one of the channels while others use a variety, changing channels depending on others' communication styles. Phone calls allow for a type of banter and possible humorous exchange that is unique

Texting became VERY popular around the turn of the century, and is still the channel of choice for getting our message across with a touch of our smartphones.

Some people only use certain channels, and don't respond at all to others. Some time ago, someone told me they hadn't heard from me and that they had texted me. This was before I was texting, and I hadn't responded because I wasn't yet on that channel. It is wise to make sure that you are reaching people on a particular channel, and use several options if you aren't certain about which channel they utilize.

What is your channel of choice? Why do you prefer it, and are you flexible and willing to use other channels if others prefer them or require it?

How Can We Use Different Channels to Reconnect with Others?

By Phone...

The phone call may seem outdated, but it is actually a wonderful way to communicate in a virtual world. There's a certain intimate nature of a phone call that really allows us to connect with someone on a deeper level. When all we have to concentrate on is their voice alone, it allows us to really listen and focus on what they are saying. Calling may actually surprise some people which is not a bad thing. It helps make you stand out, as we do live in a digital age where much of our communication happens through text or email.

Picking up the phone is a lost art and for those who embrace it consistently, it can yield wonderful benefits.

Think about the last time you received a phone call from someone you hadn't heard from in a while because they were thinking about you and just wanted to say hello. Didn't it make you feel great? You have the ability to do this with your network.

One of the greatest ways I've stayed in contact with friends from the past is calling people who I haven't talked to in a while. This allows me to rekindle the friendship that we had built. It is quite common for these phone conversations to feel similar to when I talked to this individual more frequently. As you have more and more of these conversations, you become top of mind to the people you communicate with. This will lead to more opportunities, referrals, or invitations to all kinds of activities that could create a life-changing chain of events.

The point I'm making is you never know where one phone call could lead.

Phone calls do not have to be reserved only for people that you talk to occasionally. You can set up phone calls with new people in your network as a way to get to know them better or as a way to discuss potential business opportunities. The important thing is not to discount the phone simply because it is perceived as old technology.

Another consideration is some people are a little bit more timid and may be afraid of getting on a video call or Zoom and would prefer to talk over the phone. If that is their comfort level, then it makes sense for you to honor that and allow them to interact with you in a medium where they feel most at ease.

If you do call someone out of the blue, it's always beneficial to ask if it is a good time to talk and to not hide the intention or purpose of your call. Do not wait to bring this up; instead, explain why you called immediately. If you truly just called to say hi, then let them know and continue with the conversation. But if you called because you have a referral for them or for another reason, be sure to tell them very early on in the conversation.

If you haven't talked to them in a while, they may be wondering why you are calling out of the blue. The sooner you can explain the reason, the sooner their wall will go down and they will feel more comfortable engaging in the conversation.

Regardless of the reason for your call, be sure to listen as much as you talk. Ensure the conversation has a casual back-and-forth flow so that they don't feel like it is a one directional call.

It's also a best practice to end the call by discussing next steps, such as a future meeting or a place where you can see them again (e.g. a group virtual meeting). You may even plan a potential follow-up call where you can discuss some of the topics that you weren't able to fully explore during that call.

By Text...

Perhaps one of my favorite ways to reconnect with old friends is to casually send them a text message letting them know that I am thinking about them. It is sad to know that many friendships fall by the wayside simply because both parties don't take the initiative to contact the other person. It's especially discouraging when you think about how easy it is to simply send somebody a quick text. Why then, don't we do it?

There are many psychological reasons for why we avoid reconnecting with old friends. We may think it's been too long since we've talked to them before, and we are fearful of having a conversation that may be a bit awkward. We also may be afraid of what they might think about us calling after it's been such a long time. This inner doubt is almost always self-inflicted without a justified reason or cause. I suggest testing this out by sending a text message to a few friends or colleagues you haven't spoken to in a while. The results may surprise you!

When you send them a text, be sure to let them know the reason for your text. People are fairly cynical and might be afraid that you are trying to sell them something or get them to take a look at a business opportunity. This should not be your intention of texting them as this will create immediate conflict for the majority of people. Instead, your intention should be purely to connect and let them know that you were thinking about them. I suggest being very casual in the way you write the message, letting them know that they don't need to respond right away. Once they text back, you can have a back-and-forth text conversation that may or may not lead to a subsequent phone call, Zoom meeting, or other form of conversation.

Much like a phone call with a person you haven't spoken to in a while, a text conversation can lead to potentially life-changing opportunities. This is why it is a great practice to consistently communicate even with people that you don't consider a current friend or acquaintance. This helps to expand your network and create more awareness by making you top of mind to the people who know you.

Cliques...or Bonding?

A few years ago Chris, a young member of my net-working group, lamented that the group consisted of older people who seemed to be in cliques and that he didn't feel included.

As time went by, Chris became an integral part of the group.

At meetings, Chris and I would joke around and became good friends.

I finally said to him, "Do you think people think of us a clique?" He smiled and indicated that he realized that his initial impression of feeling excluded and on the outside looking in had changed with time, and now he is actually part of the inner circle and no longer an outsider.

In fact, Chris is currently slated to be the next leader of that group.

It is an interesting phenomenon of networking or any social group that we tend to connect more with some people than others, and that cliques or groups form. Overall, bonding is a good thing, except for those who want to become assimilated into a group. It is fine to form a bond with others, but also important to include new people and invite them to be part of the group.

SOCIAL MEDIA

Harnessing the Value of Social Media

In times of social distancing, social media in general, especially LinkedIn, assumes an increased importance. You can use social media 24 hours a day, 365 days a year.

All social media platforms have potential value and allow you to connect with others even if you cannot meet in person.

LinkedIn is clearly the premier social media business platform. It doesn't cost anything except your time, effort and creativity. You can secure a Premium account for an additional monthly fee. Premium allows you increased ability to navigate the platform.

Whether you know it or like it, people who want to know about you are likely to look you up on LinkedIn. Your profile is your virtual resume, and should represent you in the best way possible.

The most important basic sections are your Banner, About section and Profile Picture. Take the time to maximize their content. Make sure that these sections are completely accurate, compelling, interesting, and free of typos.

Increase your connections and followers, the more the better. I recommend that you accept most or all connection requests, though some people recommend more selectivity.

To increase your connections, send personalized messages with each request rather than simply hitting the Connect icon. These messages should mention a reason why others would want to connect with you, and not be impersonal or standardized. Follow thought leaders, and like and comment on their posts. This will increase your visibility.

In order to derive a significant benefit from LinkedIn, Facebook, or Instagram, it is critical to post relevant and consistent content. Have conversations with others and stay engaged. Personally, I tend to use LinkedIn for business posts and Facebook for personal ones.

Facebook can also be used to post business-related information. I strongly recommend that you stay away from politics and religion. Follow business pages of others, which aids in making business relationships more personal. Facebook is an excellent place to stay in contact with others.

Twitter is a great platform to showcase your expertise (and you don't have to write a long post). Tweet about your industry using relevant hashtags. Follow hashtags that interest you, people in your field of expertise, and those from your industry. Retweet and comment on their posts. If you are more advanced with Twitter, you can use polling and live video features.

Your posts should be original and real. Don't hesitate to share personal as well as business topics. It is advantageous to show genuine vulnerability. You are not a robot, so your posts should not be bland or boring.

The Power of LinkedIn

LinkedIn provides far-and-away the best opportunity of any social media platform for networking, business development, and branding.

Chances are you have a Facebook profile and you may even have an Instagram and Twitter profile. If you think about each of those platforms, the majority of active users are sharing posts, pictures, and tweets.

LinkedIn is rare in that the vast majority of its active users don't regularly post content, which effectively creates a content deficit. Because of this, those who post content on LinkedIn are able to reach a large organic audience.

The LinkedIn feed has 9 billion content impressions every week. An "impression" is the number of times a piece of content is displayed. Only 3 million LinkedIn users post content on a weekly basis.[1] Currently, there are 690 million people on the platform[2] and LinkedIn's goal is to have 3 billion users.[1]

---

1   Josh Gallant, "58 Eye-Opening LinkedIn Stats For Marketers In 2020," Foundation Inc., last modified March 31, 2020, https://foundationinc.co/lab/b2b-marketing-linkedin-stats/.
2   Andrew Hutchinson, "LinkedIn's up to 690 Million Members, Reports 26% Growth in User Sessions," Social Media Today, April 30, 2020, https://www.socialmediatoday.com/news/linkedins-up-to-690-million-membersreports-26-growth-in-user-sessions/577067/.

One hundred million people are using the platform each day. This is significant, especially when you consider the demographic of the LinkedIn user base. Sixty-one million users have senior-level roles and 40 million are in decision-making positions. Thirty million companies can be found on LinkedIn and it's the most-used social media platform for Fortune 500 companies.[1]

LinkedIn makes up more than 50% of all social traffic from B2B websites to blogs.[1] This means if you are able to consistently post content on the platform, you could have a very large audience see your work. This will allow you to gain brand awareness, get more business, and grow your network!

LinkedIn also has an incredible global reach, with over 70% of its user base outside of the United States.[1]

Even if you decide that posting isn't your thing, LinkedIn is essentially a global networking event that is happening constantly.

Deciding how to leverage LinkedIn will be determined by your intention and mindset.

Intention

Take the time to think through what you want to achieve by being on the platform.

To start, write down 1-3 words you'd like someone to use when describing you. Basically, what words would people think of when you come to mind?

What is your primary purpose for being on LinkedIn? For example, do you want to gain brand awareness, find more clients/customers for your business, or land a dream job?

What specific metrics do you want to achieve? Do you want a certain amount of clients, sales, or interviews?

What will be your style, approach, or LinkedIn personality? Know your personality and bring it to life. Think about how you want to "show up" on the platform. What do you want to be known for?

These questions will help you solidify your goals for LinkedIn.

Mindset

The secret ingredient to maximizing LinkedIn is to have a giver's mindset. This means you approach everything by thinking about what you can give more than what you want to get out of the platform. Unfortunately, many people have a "getter's mindset" which makes it difficult to gain any traction.

A giver's mindset means you give unconditionally. When you post content, you do it to help others. When you read other's posts, you make comments. When you connect with people, you think about how you can support them. Obviously you are on LinkedIn for a reason, and clearly you will benefit from being on the platform. If you give without thinking about what you are going to get in return, you will see the reciprocity of the platform.

People appreciate the genuine kindness of givers. They are attracted to people who aren't motivated to get something from them. If you are constantly "selling" or "promoting" yourself, eventually people will tune you out.

LinkedIn Basics

In this section, I will review profile basics: Profile Picture, Headline, Banner, Contact Information, About section, Featured section, Experience, Recommendations, Endorsements, Accomplishments, and Interests.

When people click your profile it is important to remember that this is the representation of who you are.

Profile Picture

The first thing people will look at is your profile picture. We are hardwired to look at the human face before anything else. Because of this, having a great picture is imperative.

Be sure your face is well lit, you're smiling with confidence, and you're looking directly into the camera. Have a solid background that contrasts with your skin tone. You can also add a ring to the outside of your profile picture to make it pop off the page. I recommend using a design platform like Canva or hiring a freelance designer on a site like Fiverr.com to help create a profile picture that you can proudly display.

Headline

Your headline is a brief description of what you do that appears right under your name. It's important to remember that people will only give you a few seconds of their time, so your headline should clearly say what you do.

Six Ingredients for the Best Headline

1. Original. Your headline allows you to stand out from the crowd. Avoid boring statements or titles that everyone states. What makes you unique? Add humor if possible.

2. Descriptive. If you are an attorney don't just say attorney, say "patent attorney".

3. Who do you serve. Describe who your customers are. For example, "patent attorney for tech startups".

4. Searchable. Use keywords people would use to find others.

5. Personal. Say something personal about yourself.

6. Career Highlights. Do you have any accolades that sets you apart or differentiates you from everyone else? Add them.

Great Examples of Headlines

I turn your staff into content creators that generate traffic, leads, & revenue for your business 💲 DM me to learn! 💲

LinkedIn Coach | Unwavering Optimist | Classic Rock Enthusiast | LinkedIn Queen | Forbes Business Council | Personal Branding Strategist | LinkedIn Marketing

CEO 🦊 at Weatherology ⛅ Author 🖊 Podcast Host 🎙 Speaker 📣

Chairman of VaynerX, CEO of VaynerMedia, 5-Time NYT Bestselling Author

Social Media Marketing Consultant to CEO's & Entrepreneurs Influencer to 160,000 'Post to Profit' Courses Speaker

I help Execs, Coaches, & SMB's build UNFORGETTABLE BRANDS with video content.

I help designers & marketers find 80-85% of the jobs NOT posted online.

Each one of these headlines clearly states what they do and who they serve. Creating a solid headline may take a few iterations, but the best ones stand out because they are memorable, easy to understand, and descriptive.

Banner

At the very top of your LinkedIn profile is your banner. This is a lot of real estate to work with and is a common missed opportunity where people do not take advantage of making this element pop off the page. Think of it as a blank canvas that acts as your virtual business card.

What to Include in your Banner

Your personal or company mission

Description of who you serve

Your website or social media information

Credentials of professional certifications

Social proof accolades to highlight your accomplishments

Your personal hashtag

These are just ideas; you do not need to include all of these things.

You can also include imagery to help tell your story, including a picture of yourself in action. I highly recommend using a freelance designer to create a compelling banner.

Contact Information

The easier it is for people to contact you the better. Include your email address, website, social media profiles, and phone number if you don't mind calls in this section. This is key because when you transition from job to job, your email and contact information may change. By keeping this section updated, people will always be able to find you.

About Section

Your About section gives you a chance to tell your story. After seeing your profile picture, headline, and banner, it's usually the next place people look.

Your About section shouldn't regurgitate what can be found in your experience section. It should be engaging, easy to read, and have heart. What do you stand for? What makes you unique?

Since it's your story, it should be told by you, not someone else. Think as though you are telling the story directly to the person who is reading it. Don't write it in the third person.

It's important to make the About section easy to read. Avoid using long paragraphs and use as few words as possible to convey your message. Break up the content with bullets so it's easy on the eyes!

Formula for Writing a Compelling and Effective About section:

Part One: Hook

The first sentence is the hook. It has to be a super compelling statement that will grab the reader's attention. It should be bold, clear, and interesting.

It's helpful to be vulnerable and share something very personal. What major life-changing moment has helped shape who you are today? Is there a catalyst that helped you find your current job or business?

Some other ways to grab the attention of the reader is to have an opening line that asks a compelling question, a quote that represents what you stand for, or something funny that will make the reader laugh and become curious about you.

Part Two: Story

Tell your story in a creative and unique way. Be specific enough to share some of the most important highlights of your life and career, but don't include unnecessary details. Remember that others can see your experience so you don't need to tell them about every role that you've had. Instead, tell them something about the experience that stands out and/or helps to convey what sets you apart.

Part Three: Offer

This is what you offer the world. Do you have any services you provide? Be very specific about what your value or offer is and how it can benefit others. If you have specific skills or expertise that would be valuable to a potential job, then include that here. Avoid vague language that makes the reader wonder what you offer.

Part Four: Call to Action

This is the Call to Action (CTA). What do you want them to do once they've finished reading your About section? Go to your website? Schedule a meeting with you? Sign up for your newsletter?

Having a stellar About section will make people know who you are, like you, and want to get to know you even better. It is kind of like a written elevator pitch that allows you to be very open and transparent about your life story. When done effectively, your About section can make the difference between somebody connecting with you, following you, and giving you business...or NOT.

Featured Section

What do you want people to see first when it comes to your content, links, or media? If you're promoting your website, product, or service make sure that is first in your Featured section. You can also highlight your posts, images, or presentations so they stand out on your profile.

Experience

Chances are you already have this section filled out. The only question is how do you have it filled out? Does it look like a series of job descriptions? If so, then I suggest updating it to tell more of the story of how you've made an impact at each of your previous positions. Include specific metrics and numbers to help illustrate how you helped each organization you've worked for reach its goals. For example, instead of saying sales increased you can say you helped to increase sales by a specific percentage. You can also upload media, licenses, certifications, or volunteer roles in the experience section.

Recommendations

In Robert Cialdini's book, *Influence: The Psychology of Persuasion*, he highlights the importance of "Social Proof". This is a psychological phenomenon where we have a tendency to follow people based upon praise or reviews about their services or products. Think herd mentality.

I suggest asking for recommendations from people who know you really well. Co-workers, clients, employees, and managers you know will be able to provide a genuine recommendation. Who are your raving fans? Ask them first!

I also strongly suggest writing recommendations for people you've worked with in the past that you've had positive experiences with and would work with again. Don't wait for them to ask for recommendations. Take the initiative!

Ideally, you will have as many received recommendations as you do given recommendations.

Endorsements

For endorsements, it is more acceptable to go beyond only the people you worked with closely. This includes anyone who has in some way experienced your work. You don't need to know them well for them to provide an endorsement of your work. It could be a client, teammate, or acquaintance who knows of your skills and expertise.

The law of reciprocity works very well with endorsements. If you endorse people in your network who you know, it is highly likely some of them will do the same for you.

You can also proactively ask for endorsements, but only ask people who can legitimately vouch for your expertise.

Accomplishments

If you have any noteworthy accomplishments or awards, be sure to include them in this section. This feature helps create social proof for you and your talents.

Interests

When you follow thought leaders, influencers, organizations, or schools, this will show up in your interests. When people visit your profile, they will see who you follow and it will help them understand who you learn from and what you value. If you are in real estate, then following people in the real estate space will help solidify your brand as a real estate expert.

How to Communicate on LinkedIn

———

There are numerous ways to communicate on LinkedIn. It may seem like the only way to talk to someone is to send them a direct message. While a direct message is a great means of communication, it is most certainly not the only way we can communicate. In this section we will discuss all the various ways to communicate with people on LinkedIn, starting with how to find the right people to communicate with. Then we will discuss how to send personalized connection requests, how build relationships through messages, how to engage in posts with thoughtful comments, and how to create meaningful content that helps to communicate who you are and what value you provide.

Making Strategic Connections

Ideally, you want to connect with people who are active on LinkedIn. If they are engaging in other people's content, then chances are they will engage with your content.

To target even more specifically, find people in your industry who are actively posting on LinkedIn and who are getting good engagement in their posts. When you find these people, follow them or connect with them, and then regularly comment on their posts. Like and comment on other people's comments within those same posts and then send connection requests to those people. If they are commenting already, chances are they will also comment on your posts, especially if it is about topics they find interesting. If you are in real estate, for example, find people who regularly post about real estate and engage in their posts.

In order to find people in your industry or field of interest, use the search bar, follow hashtags related to your space, and identify Influencers in your industry.

Sending Personalized Connection Requests

You can blindly connect with people on LinkedIn by sending a connection request without a personalized message. While this approach may increase connection count, this is not the best way to build genuine relationships. To network and actually meet people, it is best to start off with a thoughtful, personalized note.

Connection Request Formula

1. Common Ground. Review their profile and look for areas of commonality, infusing humor if you can.

"I noticed you're a ramen lover like me."

2. Pay a Compliment. Be specific and genuine.

"I really liked your comment on Jay Abbasi's recent post about mindfulness."

3. Enthusiastic Ask. Make the connection request statement.

"I'd love to connect if you're open to it."

4. Stand Out. Say who you are, what have you done, and what you're doing.

"To introduce myself...I led sales training for Tesla globally and now host a business podcast called Insight Out."

Using this formula will vastly increase the chance that people will accept your request. It also establishes a great first impression and sets up the beginning of a relationship.

Building Relationships with Direct Messages (DM)

Being able to effectively engage via direct message is without question, one of the most important components of building a network on LinkedIn. The better you get to know someone, the more likely you are to build a relationship with them. While you can get to know someone through comments and by reading their content, a direct message is more personal and is a great lead-in to a video chat or in-person meeting.

It is important to be as authentic and natural as possible. An easy way to ensure you're being genuine is to pretend like you're talking to the person face-to-face. The more casual and conversational you are, the more people will see you as a "normal" person. Imagine you're at a backyard BBQ having a conversation, not talking to a computer.

It starts by using a conversational tone. Short, casual dialogue works a lot better than long copying and pasting blurbs that make it obvious you spent little to no time thinking about the other person. When people receive something that isn't personalized, they think they can ignore it. This doesn't mean you can't copy and paste parts of your messages, but it should be blended with personal touches so that it makes the other person feel special. Draw on things from their profile or from previous messages to bring up topics that they'll want to talk about. People love talking about themselves, so casually ask questions about them.

Be careful because it's easy to make it seem forced or disingenuous. Rather than picking the easiest thing to talk about that is obvious from their headline or job title, try to find something that others wouldn't even notice. For example, when reading the about section or looking at their experience, is there anything that stands out that is unique or different? Find areas of common ground, like education, profession, locations you've both lived in, or similar interests.

It's also easy to be somewhat annoying if you overdo this. No one likes it when someone comes on too strong, as we naturally have defense mechanisms that make us skeptical of what others want from us. Your conversation should aim to lower the walls people normally have, which will ultimately lead to them trusting you. Another great way to build trust is to share something personal about yourself. Vulnerably sharing something about yourself can endear others to you like a magnet, and it is a great way to build a bond!

Avoid pleasantries that seem forced or stale. Instead, say something that's a bit more unique and shows your personality. This is your chance to win them over and make them like you, which will take a while if you're asking about the weather. It's better to surprise them by asking them something unique.

Some people are not into messaging or don't have the time to really engage. If you're talking to a person with a large following, chances are they are inundated with messages and may not want to have a long conversation with you right off the bat.

Do not waste time having conversations with the wrong people. You are likely to receive countless sales pitches on LinkedIn. If you're not careful, these will suck the time out of your day if you let them.

Another excellent way to connect is by using the voice message feature. It is especially helpful to send a voice message after first connecting with someone. It is much more personal as they can hear your voice and start to get to know you more than if you just send a text message. You can also send a personalized introduction video to help make you stand out from the crowd.

Direct messaging allows you to get to know the people in your network. If you really hit it off with someone, you can graduate your relationship by taking it off-platform and meeting them in person, on a video call, or phone call. This will take your relationship to the next level and help you truly connect with people in your LinkedIn network.

Engaging in Posts

One of the most powerful ways to build an organic network is to engage in other people's content. This is where the "giver's mindset" is most needed. Your feed, which is where you see all the posts, is a compilation of content from a variety of sources, including from people in your network and people whose content has been liked or commented on by someone in your network. You should regularly scroll through your feed to find posts that strike a chord with you and inspire you to share your take on what is being said. Be sure to click one of the emotion buttons (like, love, etc.) and then leave a comment that adds value to the conversation.

When you make a comment, think of it as an opportunity to share your ideas, expertise, and authentic self. Each comment you make is like a piece of micro-content, and you want that content to be just as impactful as any posts you make.

Avoid making comments that add little to no value like "Great post!", "Thanks for sharing!", "I love your work!", "Cool!", "Nice share!", " ".

Also avoid making comments that are generic, boring, self-promoting, or mean-spirited.

Be sure to read the entire post to make sure you truly understand and then add your comment.

Comments are a great opportunity to add value to the conversation and will lead people to want to get to know you better.

Breakdown of a Great Comment

1. Compliment. Say thank you or in some way let them know you appreciate their post.

2. Take away. Mention what you learned by reading/viewing the post.

3. Your Take. What is your insight or perspective on the topic that is discussed?

4. Tag. Tag the author and anyone who would contribute to the conversation or be interested.

5. Memorable. Make your comment stand out by making it original in some way or by infusing humor.

6. Be Kind. Be polite and courteous, and avoid any language that can be misconstrued.

Key Tips for Engaging in Posts

1. Use the "@" symbol to tag the author. They get a notification when you do this and it also shows more of a personal touch.

2. Edit the comment. Click the ellipses in the top right corner to do so.

3. Always like your comments. This will give your comment a greater chance of being seen by others.

4. Use emojis. These add emphasis, emotion, and humor.

5. Use GIF or images. By using other media, your comments will stand out.

Creating Content:

There is no perfect way to make content. However, here is a four-part formula that will help create consistency and allow you to deliver a message that provides value to the reader.

Part 1: The Hook

Get attention by making a bold statement or asking a question that will stop people from scrolling and make it so they can't resist reading MORE!

Part 2: The Story

People love listening to stories and it helps to make the concept you're sharing easy to understand and relatable. If the story is personal and from the heart, people will connect with you! Share personal stories to draw the interest of the reader.

Part 3: The Value

A personal story is nice, but people are wondering "What's in it for me(WIFM)?" What's the key message or take-away you want the audience to remember? Provide something of value that is applicable, like a skill or helpful knowledge.

Part 4: Call to Action

Ask the reader to take the next step. For example, ask them to make a comment, ask a question to inspire them and join the conversation, or remind them about your services. Be careful of over-promoting yourself. It should be casual and not "salesy".

It is also important to remember to make the post as digestible as possible. Space out the paragraphs so that you only have one or three sentences per paragraph. It is also helpful to infuse humor and make the post stand out by providing valuable information in a novel way. You are competing with all the other content out there, so think about what will make your post stand out from the rest!

Your content should empower the reader by providing knowledge to help them become better in their field. Think of your post like a school. In a sense, you are providing education to the reader. Share what you're reading or any ideas, concepts, or insights you have about your industry. You want to be seen as a trusted and safe expert they can depend on as a resource. Answer the question, what would my audience want to learn? What will resonate with them? Then share based on that.

Hashtags:

One of the best ways to allow your content to gain more visibility is by including hashtags in your posts. Hashtags have become ubiquitous within social media, and every platform uses hashtags to help organize content.

When you assign a hashtag to your post, it allows other people that are following that hashtag to potentially see your content. Think of it like a flag you hold in the air in a crowd so people can find you. It is commonly understood that if you follow a hashtag and someone else in your network also follows that same hashtag, then that piece of content is more likely to show up in their feed.

People also have the ability to type in the hashtag directly into the search bar, and your content will be included in the posts that show up for that specific hashtag. A common mistake is that people include hashtags in their posts that are not followed by very many people. I advise picking two hashtags that have high follower counts to include in each post.

Not all hashtags are created equal. For example, #personaldevelopment and #personalgrowth may sound similar, but the former has 14,792,657 followers and the latter has 5,789 followers. The algorithm looks favorably when you and your followers are following the same hashtag, and since they are more likely to follow a high follower hashtag, it makes sense to use that one.

Do your own due diligence and research on the hashtag before including it in your post. You can see how many followers a hashtag has by entering it into the search bar.

It's important that they relate to the content you are sharing. In other words, don't put #Mindfulness if the post is about podcasting. It is widely believed that you should use no more than three hashtags in a post. Think about hashtags like you would think about hot sauce. A little bit goes a long way!

Personal Hashtags

Personal hashtags help to build personal brand! It reminds people of your area of expertise, consolidates all of your content in one place, and helps the algorithm increase the visibility of your posts.

If a connection of yours follows your hashtag, it will give your post an extra boost. It's important that you remember to follow your own personal hashtag for this very reason.

Anything could be your personal hashtag. You just need to think of a phrase that best represents you. It could be your actual name or branding for your business/service.

It's important to make it personal/unique to YOU - not broad topics like #Marketing or #SocialMedia. You should check to make sure someone else isn't using the same hashtag as well.

Once you've identified the word(s) you want to use, simply put a hashtag in front of it. You can include it in the body of your posts, share it with people via DM, and add it to your headline, banner, and about section.

Tagging:

Tagging someone in your post is commonly done to inform people of the content you just posted. Think of it like you tapping them on the shoulder and saying, "Hey, check this out, I think you may like it!"

It's also done when responding to comments, and it is considered polite to reference somebody's name when commenting. It's widely believed the algorithm likes it when there is reciprocated tagging from both the author of the post and the people who he or she tags.

Typically when you type the "@" symbol, LinkedIn will give you options of names to include as a tag, and as you type out more letters, those options will change.

It's not advisable to arbitrarily tag dozens of people simply to get them to look at your post.

An advantage that you will find by tagging people in the comments of your post is that it may result in them liking or commenting on your posts. This is especially helpful during the first hour after posting.

LinkedIn Algorithm

Understanding the algorithm can make the difference between your posts gaining traction or not. Unfortunately, LinkedIn does not publish how their algorithm works so theories have been pieced together based on personal analysis of people who study it and on limited information revealed by the company. The way in which the algorithm works has changed a lot throughout the years!

Regardless of the changes in the algorithm, it is a safe bet that LinkedIn wants people to be active on their platform. This fundamental truth means that if you are regularly posting and making comments, it will always be deemed as positive in the eyes of the "LinkedIn Gods".

It is widely believed that the LinkedIn algorithm assigns a quality score to your content before it is sent to your connections and followers. Based on that assessment, it will send your content to a small group to see how it performs. Based on how engaged people are on your post during this initial phase, the algorithm will determine if your post should be sent to a wider audience. When someone likes or comments on your post, it will show in the feed of some of the people who follow them.

LinkedIn expert Andy Foote[3] says we should think of the likes and comments of your post like a pinball machine. Engagement in your content act like the flippers or bumper that keep the ball in play. Likes, mentions, comments, and re-shares all help keep the post alive and active much like the flippers and bumpers keep your pinball game going!

This is especially important during the first hour after a post is released. If no one reacts or comments on your posts within the first hour after posting, it will perform badly and get low engagement and views. Conversely, if there's a lot of activity in the first hour of the post, it will likely reach a larger audience. It is important to note that you can also contribute to the early engagement by replying to any comments on your post. This is an easy and important way to ensure your post is bouncing around that pinball machine in the first hour! Comments seem to be the biggest factor that helps to make a post perform well.

Over-posting can harm the reach of your posts. This means you should avoid posting back-to-back and instead wait at least a few hours before posting something new. It is also believed that native videos are far better than including links to YouTube, which will push people away from the platform.

---

3   Andy Foote, "The LinkedIn Algorithm Explained In 25 Frequently Asked Questions," LinkedIn Insights, Sept. 5, 2019, https://www.linkedinsights.com/the-linkedin-algorithm-explained-in-25-frequently-asked-questions/.

While we don't know exactly how LinkedIn evaluates the quality of a post, one thing seems to be very consistent: posts that showcase authenticity seem to fare far better. Anyone can post information, but only you can share your personal viewpoint and thoughts. No matter what the algorithm does or doesn't do, the most important thing to remember is be yourself.

APPLICATIONS AND THE FUTURE

Virtual Meetings: Other Groups

Many groups have taken to Zoom technology to meet when face-to-face meeting is still prohibited. Service organizations like Rotary, book clubs, families, and friends are jumping on the Zoom bandwagon in increasing numbers.

These types of meetings, welcomed by some, have had mixed reviews. While many people are happy to have them, others eschew virtual meetings and opt to wait until we are free to meet in person.

One of the main challenges and limitations of virtual meetings is the sheer size of the group, especially when some people dominate the conversation. If there is not a leader or moderator, the discussions can be unwieldy. Some people are still at the "honeymoon" stage with Zoom, and groups are learning to set some guidelines.

Another major issue with virtual get togethers and meetings is how long they should be and when to terminate them. In-person troikas have a natural ending point when the bill comes. Virtual meetings have no such termination point. The length could be determined in advance by the meeting organizer.

Whether the meeting is a troika, a business meeting, or a social get together, we need to develop some guidelines in order for them to have value.

Rotary Club

The Rotary Club of Ventura started meeting weekly via Zoom in March.

Prior to the pandemic, this club had about 50 members attending per week at the Derby Club at the Ventura Fairgrounds. It was a lunch meeting, and prior to lunch there was the wearing of name badges, hand shaking and mingling. Food was served buffet style, and there was a speaker.

On Zoom, the meetings are quite different. Attendance has dropped to an average of about 30 attendees and not everyone speaks. Some of the older members who lack technical skills are not attending the Zoom meetings.

There are mixed feelings about the virtual meetings. Though it does allow members to connect virtually, it is clearly not the same. The in-person meetings had a quality that is difficult to replicate via Zoom.

The club recently held a very successful socially distanced, masked, outdoor social event in a large setting to allow club members to meet face-to-face.

Book Club

It is useful to consider groups other than networking groups to gain some perspective and comparisons.

The book club I am considering is a group of 14 women who have been meeting in person for over 40 years. They are all former professionals (lawyers, judges, psychologists, professors, writers, designers).

The group is highly successful and intelligent. They enjoyed meeting once a month at members' homes on a rotating basis, with dinner provided by the host.

COVID hit and they pivoted to Zoom meetings.

All of sudden there was no driving, arranging car pools, preparing dinner for the group, and assembling for the meeting.

Everyone called in at 6 p.m. and talked in order about the chosen book. There were no side conversations. There was one conversation, and everyone took their turn to speak. It wasn't the same. One person opined that the quieter people seemed to talk more than they did at in-person meetings. Not everyone loved Zoom, but attendance is better than ever.

Everyone left the meeting at the same time. There was no discussion in car pools on the way home, but there was at least some connection.

Mah Jongg

Four women play Mah Jongg every Tuesday at 1 p.m., rotating each week from one player's home to another. Food is served, and the game is played for about 3 hours. They meet in person...or so they did.

When the pandemic first hit, they didn't play at all in person and didn't see each other in person.

A couple of them discovered online Mah Jongg, and others learned it.

Now they play together online every Tuesday at 1 p.m., connecting on the app Duo.

It is not the same. There is minimal conversation between games; there are no hugs nor food, a previous centerpiece of the games. It is better than nothing, but less than ideal.

Virtual Networking Meetings: The Future

Nobody knows exactly what the future holds in terms of the status of in-person vs. virtual networking. We do know that we can hold Zoom meetings indefinitely, as long as we have internet connection. Networking groups can refocus and change their membership guidelines and fees. What we don't know is the possibility and feasibility of "hybrid" meetings, wherein some people are allowed to attend in person and others must attend virtually from remote locations.

Many people enjoy and prefer in-person meetings, and are counting the days when we return to the way things were pre-COVID. They have opined that there is no substitute for meeting in person, shaking others' hands, hugging those that they are closer to, and breaking bread (or bagels) together. From my discussions and research with a number of groups, the strong proponents of in-person meetings over virtual is decreasing as people become more comfortable with Zoom and treasure the time saved from not driving to meetings.

Let me share my own thoughts honestly and directly. I live in the city of Ventura, which is over 50 miles away from my closest group meeting in Encino, and another 20 miles to the other one I lead in Downtown Los Angeles. I love being a Group Leader in those two groups, and attending my other "home" Provisors group in Sherman Oaks. But I don't love driving in heavy traffic, looking for parking, and going through Security. I don't mind getting up early, but I would be content if Zoom meetings continued indefinitely. Though I don't really look forward to the return to far away morning networking meetings, I really like the people in my groups and like seeing them in person. If the groups I lead decided to become total Zoom groups, I would be totally okay with it.

Another persistent and nagging question, perhaps a more basic one, is what will be the policy of hosting firms in terms of social distancing and the number of people allowed in a room. As this is being written in August 2020, the various firms' management are considering such decisions. Of course, the decision about how many employees can be present in an office take priority over the acceptable capacity for networking meetings.

For now, it is premature to assume exactly what will happen, how it will happen, and when it will happen.

There are more questions than answers, such as:

> **How important is it (really) to be at the meeting in person?**
>
> **If Zoom meetings continue, how will the geographic reach of networking groups change?**
>
> **Will people remain in networking groups if attending in person is not easy?**
>
> **Are in-person meetings fundamentally superior to Zoom meetings?**
>
> **Would people still prefer in-person meetings if they had to wear masks or face coverings in order to attend?**

Some people and groups are still quite anxious to get back to "normal", that is, meeting in person. That day can't come soon enough for them. They love their group, their meeting location and all that goes with it. They have a clear and adamant preference for meeting in person and given a choice, would return to that format.

What is your opinion? Would you prefer to meet in-person, or could you derive an equal (or better) overall value by continuing with Zoom meetings?

There is little doubt that we won't soon (or ever) return to large, often crowded in-person meetings. This reality is slowly being accepted by increasing numbers of people.

Unique Time in History

We are in a unique time in history.

The COVID-19 pandemic is still raging, which is unlike anything we have seen in our lifetimes. This situation is arguably the most challenging for individual lives. It eclipses 9/11 in terms of the daily impact. Although 9/11 was monumental in terms of lives lost on a single day and security changes, COVID-19 has impacted the way we ALL live for months and might continue to do so.

Concurrently, we are seeing a vast increase in awareness of longtime racial injustice, particularly the Black Lives Matter movement, which accelerated following the multiple killing of unarmed citizens.

So we have a global pandemic and racial reckoning, along with continuous debates about which statues and monuments should be removed.

These are the best of times and the worst of times, depending on your particular life and how you want to focus.

Conclusion

The COVID-19 pandemic has changed the way we live and work in many ways, and things are still evolving as this is being written. The virus is still spreading, and people are still dying. It is a profoundly sad and uncertain time. We will undoubtedly be in a virtual world of interpersonal communication in general and networking specifically for awhile.

One thing is certain, and that is that we should remain flexible. It is highly unlikely that things will return to the way they were in February. Many signs point to the likelihood of a hybrid world at work, in education, in networking and with a variety of other social groups.

The real goal of networking is to build mutually beneficial relationships over time, whether we meet in person or not. Human beings have a remarkable ability to adapt and an insatiable desire to connect in a meaningful way with others. Continue to be open to the various ways that we can reach others.

Focus on reality! Though you might prefer meeting in person, we are all facing a situation that will not be like it was prior to the pandemic, at least for an unknown period of time. Embrace the incredible technology we have, and learn to use it effectively. There are a multitude of benefits in the virtual world, and you should utilize the limitless possibilities that enable us to connect. Can we still connect when we can't meet in person? The answer is a resounding YES!! We have already been doing it now for months and will continue to do so into the future. Technology is here to stay, and virtual communication should become an integral part of our connecting toolkit.

When all is said and done, connecting is connecting, whether in person, on Zoom, or some other channel. As our society continues to change, it is wise to accurately assess the value of each form to you and to be willing to accept situations that might be novel. Connect with others in any way you can. Your life will be richer for doing so.

Also by William M. Saleebey

Connecting: Key Networking Tips for Business and Life

Connecting: Beyond the Name Tag

Sell Yourself

Study Skills for Success

Biography

Dr. Bill Saleebey is a foremost expert on the psychological and practical aspects of business and personal networking. He is the author of the books *Connecting: Key Networking Tips for Business and Life*, *Connecting: Beyond the Name Tag*, *Sell Yourself*, and *Study Skills for Success*. He has been speaking, training and teaching on a wide variety of topics since 1972. Dr. Saleebey received his Ph.D. in Education with a specialization in Counseling from UCLA in 1980. He serves as a consultant and trainer with businesses to infuse networking into their business development practices.

Dr. Saleebey's diverse career has included research on the educational problems of Samoan migrants based on his work on the island of American Samoa which was the basis of his doctoral dissertation, the creation and development of the Study Skills Seminar, and over thirty-eight years of business development experience as a relocation manager, currently with MSI. He facilitates networking groups with ProVisors where he is a Group Leader, and Bruin Professionals. He is past President of Bruin Professionals and current Group Leader of the BP Encino chapter.

Dr. Saleebey is a keynote speaker, networking coach, business development trainer for corporations, and teaches group leaders how to facilitate the group process. He works with professional firms, educational institutions and a wide variety of businesses to implement effective networking skills into business. His work also includes forming and nurturing the growth of networking groups in industry and with alumni organizations.

APPENDICES

APPENDIX A: Brief History of Business Networking in Southern California

Business networking in an informal sense has been around forever.

Networking was done in service clubs like Rotary, Lions and Kiwanis. It was also done at churches and synagogues. People networked in many places to build relationships, obtain business and develop a community.

BNI was founded by Dr. Ivan Misner in 1985. The first group was in Arcadia, California. Formal business networking as such can be definitely marked at least partly with the establishment of Professionals Network Group, also known as PNG, in 1988. The original founders of PNG were Davis Blaine, a Mergers and Acquisition investment banker with Mentor Group, and Eric Shaw, a lender with New York Credit who was part of the original group.

Eric left PNG after a couple years and was replaced by Gordon Gregory, an investment banker with Mosaic Capital. Originally, PNG was less of a formal business networking group and more of a financial business deal group. There was originally just a couple of chapters. The Encino chapter was run by Gordon, and Davis led one in Westlake.

PNG changed its name to Provisors around 2010. I remembering telling Davis that I thought PNG was a great brand. He responded, "We are changing it to Provisors."

Eric Shaw started his own networking group, All Cities Resource Group, in 1992. It was patterned after PNG/Provisors. All Cities currently has about 400 members and charges $850 per year.

Randy Sheinbein is a commercial real estate broker and UCLA alum. He was a member of All Cities, and broke off to form Bruin Professionals in 2002 with co-founders Mike Anderson, Matt Baker and Mark Baker. Bruin Professionals currently has 11 chapters, 250 members, and charges $425 per year.

Davis's son, Justin Blaine started Athletes Touch in 2009, a business networking organization comprised of ex-collegiate and former professional athletes. They have about 250 members. Their membership fee is $1,000 per year.

Forrest Blake, a commercial real estate broker, started Highrise Networks, patterned after Provisors, in 2015. They charge $150/month.

Provisors' current CEO is Matt Toledo, former editor of the LA Business Journal. Provisors currently has over 210 groups nationally and over 6,000 members. Their yearly membership fee is $1,800.

There was another very significant networking presence in Los Angeles. A man named Carl Terzian, who ran a public relations firm, started a series of networking lunches that he personally invited people to attend. The significant, unique feature was Carl's query about the "back of the business card". Carl passed away in 2016. I am not certain if they have continued, as they were very much tied to Carl himself.

APPENDIX B: Bruin Professionals Zoom Survey Results

Bruin Professionals surveyed its members to gauge their experience on Zoom for the past six months. The majority of members (89%) viewed their experience as very or somewhat positive and indicated that they preferred a speaker as the main program for the meeting. Although people enjoyed networking with the whole group, people definitely preferred breakout rooms and have enjoyed getting to know each other in a more intimate setting. Members have greatly liked the convenience of Zoom meetings, and the time they save in the morning or afternoon. They also have appreciated meeting people in lesser known geographic areas and still being able to connect amidst the pandemic. The large meeting sizes, lack of face-to-face interaction, multi-tasking, and people dominating the conversation have lessened attendees' satisfaction with Zoom.

As of now, virtual troikas are the norm as most people are uncomfortable with in-person meetings. In the future, most members (92%) opted for at least one meeting for each chapter per year to stay on Zoom, showing how this technology has blossomed and is here to stay.

Made in the USA
Las Vegas, NV
08 March 2021

19250989R00115